Coherent Self, Coherent World:

a new synthesis of Myth, Metaphysics
& Bohm's Implicate Order
Reclaiming Value in a Fractured Age

Coherent Self, Coherent World:

a new synthesis of Myth, Metaphysics
& Bohm's Implicate Order
Reclaiming Value in a Fractured Age

Diana Durham

BOOKS
Winchester, UK
Washington, USA

JOHN HUNT PUBLISHING

First published by O-Books, 2019
O-Books is an imprint of John Hunt Publishing Ltd., 3 East St., Alresford,
Hampshire SO24 9EE, UK
office@jhpbooks.net
www.johnhuntpublishing.com

For distributor details and how to order please visit the 'Ordering' section on our website.

Design: Cecilia Perriard

UK: Printed and bound by CPI Group (UK) Ltd, Croydon, CR0 4YY
US: Printed and bound by Thomson-Shore, 7300 West Joy Road, Dexter, MI 48130

Unless attributed, all poems or extracts of poems at the chapter headings are by the author.

We operate a distinctive and ethical publishing philosophy in
all areas of our business, from our global network of authors to
production and worldwide distribution.

Contents

Other Books by Diana Durham:

Non-fiction:
The Return of King Arthur: Completing the Quest for Wholeness,
Inner Strength, and Self-Knowledge
Jeremy P. Tarcher/Penguin 2004
ISBN 1-58542-297-5

Fiction:
The Curve of the Land
Skylight Press 2015
ISBN 978-1-908011-92-3

Poetry:
Sea of Glass
The Diamond Press 1989
ISBN 0-948684-06-2

To the End of the Night
Northwoods Press 2004
ISBN 0-89002-374-3

Between Two Worlds
Chrysalis Poetry 2014

Perceval & the Grail in CD and downloadable form as an
audioplay as well as an animated series on YouTube Perceval &
the Grail Part 1 Morgana's Retelling – YouTube (https://www.
youtube.com/watch?v=EGv8MiZkkFQ&t=3s). Her channel
also features a series of talks about *Coherence & the Grail Myth*:
https://youtu.be/uNG1Oceom_A

More information at: www.dianadurham.net

For Jonathan, whose generous love and support
made the writing of this work possible.

Introduction

The Whole Self Produces Whole Outcomes

The genuine coherence of our ideas does not come from the reasoning that ties them together, but from the spiritual impulse that gives rise to them.
Nicolás Gómez Dávila

Coherence means the quality of forming a unified whole. We experience coherence in relationship with a caring partner, a close friend or mentor. These relationships are balanced, reciprocal. We are each different individuals, but we have a sense of meaningful relatedness, one which nurtures and expands the fundamental sense of ourself. We feel part of a unified whole. We can also experience coherence when we walk through buildings that have been well-designed. We respond to the proportions of their physical space, and are able to find our way around with ease, feeling on both counts again a sense of meaningful relationship. And we may find the way someone writes or speaks coherent. Their ideas are logically consistent and hold together, their arguments are clear and make sense so that we understand what they mean.

But the cornerstone of coherence is the experience of being a unified whole in our own right as individuals. This is a potential available to us as human beings because we have two aspects to our identity or two qualities of awareness. We have an inner presence, and an outer or personality self. While any words we use to talk about identity and the self are naturally subject to many different interpretations, for simplicity's sake, I will for the most part refer to these two aspects of ourselves as the inner self, and the personality self. And in this book I want to show how it is the meaningful relationship between these two that opens the space of coherence in us, with its percolating lift of relief and perspective, which then leads to coherence in how we think and what we create.

The modern West mostly ignores the presence of our inner self, so that its potential lurks like the proverbial elephant in the room that no one talks about. Only this elephant is not just in a room, it is in the entire social and cultural world we inhabit. Alan Watts described this syndrome as a taboo: 'The most strongly enforced of all known taboos is the taboo against knowing who or what you really are...' from *The Book: On the Taboo Against Knowing Who You Are*.

To acknowledge the inner self goes against a prevailing orthodoxy that takes its cue from scientific reductionism which sees the world as material only, including human beings. According to this view, our minds, emotions and personalities are just electrical firings in the brain cells. Scientific reductionism has coalesced out of interpretations of the theory of evolution, psychology and genetics. The end result is the notion that we, like the rest of the flora and fauna, are biological survival mechanisms, driven by the imperative of genes that want to reproduce themselves.

But this interpretation of the life sciences has not kept pace with the discoveries of quantum physics which showed, over a hundred years ago, that matter is not simply material because at the subatomic level particles appear to be temporary waves appearing and disappearing out of a vast ocean of deeper energy. Therefore the advance guard of science, which is physics, tells us that something else is in the mix, and that all of matter is interwoven with an energetic or non-material aspect. And on this basis alone, the scientific reductionist approach is incoherent because it is not logically consistent with the findings of physics.

In my own experience, the existence of a deeper aspect of myself has always been obvious, and characterizing humans as highly complex biological survival systems seems a bizarrely narrow view. But more importantly, I believe that because this view is incoherent, it leads to incoherence in our thought and actions both as individuals and as a society. This is because it conditions us to think of ourselves as what I term the personality self only, defined by the sum total of the nature and nurture elements allotted to us. As a result, we mostly override the presence of our inner self, discount its promptings and thereby drain life of its deeper meaning.

My aim is to explain why the inner self is the crucial aspect of our identity, and the key to our happiness and effectiveness as human beings. I look at how accessing the inner self affects the way we perceive the world, and therefore the way we impact it. I show that the balanced relationship between inner and outer selves is the loom of our creativity in every field – including our ideas, our art and design, our relationships and our leadership. Conversely, I also analyse the subtle steps involved when identity, focussed in the personality self only, feels fearful and inflates, leading to Narcissism, the abuse of power and the depletion of values.

Most social sciences participate in the bias against awareness of the inner self. With a few exceptions, notably psychosynthesis, psychotherapy is the obedient offspring of psychology, and follows the materialist orthodoxy viewing human beings as assailed by different degrees of personality disorders. Moreover, it is believed that some of the (ever lengthening) list of disorders, such as alcoholism, may be helped along by genetic propensities. So in order to find insight about this part of ourselves (other than our own experience as we start to notice it) we have to refer to ancient myth and sacred texts. This is because the two-fold nature of our identity – the 'human' bit and the 'being' bit – and the relationship between them forms the essential teaching of the wisdom traditions, both East and West. Moreover, it is also the meaning encoded in many mythic archetypes. In this book I pick and choose from strands of all these ingredients, using a mix of symbols, including sacred geometry, and texts that I am familiar with, and translating or 'decoding' them into terms understandable today. Therefore, the range of references is eclectic and not meant to be comprehensive, although I suspect that most, if not all, of the ancient sacred traditions and mythic archetypes contain essentially the same information about ourselves. They comprise our operating instructions.

However, I make a distinction between these sources and the body of belief that has grown up around the world's major religions, which have become dominated for the most part by *beliefs about* metaphysical concepts. In the process, the potential of an *experienced* relationship with a deeper dimension of oneself has been largely forgotten. This potential was explained with remarkable brevity, for instance, in the phrases: 'My Father and I are one'; 'it is not ye that speak, but the Spirit of your Father which speaketh in you'; 'The Father within, he doeth the works'. Whether we interpret 'Father' as the inner self or a larger entity called god doesn't really matter. The point is, he/she/the deeper self is 'within'. And there is the potential to 'be one' with this inner dimension. But for me there is a big difference between these sayings of Jesus (however accurately or inaccurately translated) and the vast edifice of belief that has been built upon them. Mainly because this edifice is formed around the idea that Jesus had a unique relationship to the 'Father', which is not so easily available to everyone else. In other words, the very opposite of what I believe he meant.

In Hindu, Buddhist and Chinese systems of thought, a more complex vocabulary about this relationship was evolved, defining layers of transcendent consciousness such as Atman, Buddha-nature and Shen. In the grail myth, there is the figure of the Grail King, an elderly man with white hair who lives in the inner room of the Grail Castle, and whose nature is so refined he can live on the white wafers served to him from the grail. The Grail King in his inner room is a symbol of the same dimension of identity that Jesus called 'My Father'. But when Perceval first finds his way into the Grail Castle, he does not yet realize that the Grail King lives there.

The inner dimension of self, however languaged, however we may or may not have thought about it, constitutes an immediate, in-the-moment dimension that we can access, directly, for ourselves at any moment we choose to do so. There is nothing mysterious or mystical about it. But, like Perceval, we may have to become consciously aware of its existence.

In addition to the insights from ancient texts and myth, I draw on the work of theoretical physicist David Bohm, whose profound grasp of quantum theory and its implications helped him evolve a radical new understanding of reality which involved a deeper order of interiority within the universe itself, and a dynamic process of evolution and creativity in which human beings participated.

While mainstream academia is still dominated by the materialist orthodoxy, teachers of practical spirituality abound in today's society, and precepts to do with mindfulness and balance are finding their way into the language and curricula of self-help gurus, executive coaches and consultants by the armload. Yet despite these inroads, 'spirituality' is still often talked about as if it is an optional extra, or a hobby, or simply a method of relaxation. My aim is to show it is none of these. Connecting to our inner self is fundamental to thinking and perceiving coherently, and therefore effectively. The whole self gives rise to whole outcomes: in moral, aesthetic and practical terms. It is what will facilitate the wider renewal of culture and a balanced approach to use of resources and the environment. This is not an optional extra, it is the only way forward.

Chapter 1

Who Am I?

The seat of the soul is where the inner world and the outer world meet.
Where they overlap, it is in every point of the overlap.
Novalis

Two Worlds
Life is all relationship after all –
It's like this: there are two worlds, one inner
one outer, we are in both and neither,
which may sound difficult but is simple.

We are the overlap, the connection,
that which is pours through us, we give it names:
love, power, wisdom they all mean the same
then we shape this into our creation.

The relationship between these two realms
grows meaning, just as all those other dreams
of love and marriage – fields for our desires
to be seeded. And everything conspires

to expand, like space, like flower fractals
cobwebs, lace – knitting more out of itself.

The sign in London's Science Museum asked, 'WHO AM I?' in giant blue neon letters. It was the title of an exhibit on genetics, neuroscience and psychology. Large semi-transparent walls were patterned with pairs of chromosomes and the alphabet of their DNA sequence; glass display cases explained, among other things, how new DNA testing proved Thomas Jefferson had fathered a child with one of his slaves; and interactive digital games showed the way life expectancy varies according to the behavioural patterns that arise from our genes, neurology and cultural conditioning. In other words, the answer to the question was that I am the product of the interaction between my genes, my brain and my cultural background. But having my identity defined so clearly and definitely made it all the more evident to me, as I stood looking around, stimulated by the displays, watching other people, spinning through thought processes, enjoying the whole experience, that I am also something else. Something that cannot be so easily defined.

Not for the first time I reflected on the pleasure of being present, and of knowing a depth of presence that I live from and in. This presence is like a source of myself, and is something that I have found to be just as influential in the way I live as genetic or cultural factors. This source does not appear to have any end to it and exists outside of time in the 'present' moment. When we die, we are no longer there as containers of it in the experience of our family and friends, but whether there is an absolute end to our presence cannot be proven one way or another. So we have this presence that is not dimensional and we have a personality self that has a body and lives in the dimensional world. We have two aspects to ourselves, with two corresponding qualities of awareness.

In order to think about invisible and intangible subjects such as our inner self and our consciousness it is helpful to use visible symbols. And the symbol I use throughout this book to think about our two-fold identity is the shape created out of two intersecting, equal circles:

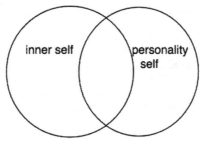

This symbol is millennia old, and was used in the early civilizations of Mesopotamia, Africa and Asia to depict the meeting of heaven and earth through which life was first made. Heaven and earth are a poetic way of talking about the inner and the outer, the undimensional and the manifest. It was taken for granted that all things grew out of the interaction between an invisible order and the visible. This symbol is most commonly known today as the *vesica piscis*, Latin for vessel of the fish, or the mandorla, meaning almond, both named for the shape created by the circles' overlap.

In Buddhist teaching a cosmology of consciousness was evolved that centred around this relationship of inner and outer identity. Lama Anagarika Govinda, a Western exponent of Tibetan Buddhism, wrote that when we are aware of our inner presence, we are allowing the quality of what he called 'intuitive mind' to emerge which he defined as the overlapping of the 'universal spiritual' and the 'empirical individual':

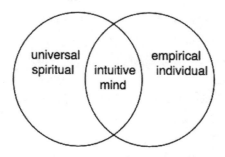

In other words, intuitive mind is created out of the relationship between two aspects of self, just as the fish or almond shape in the middle of the vesica piscis symbol is created out of the relationship between two circles. The symbol is a unified whole, made possible by the meaningful relationship of its component parts, and it demonstrates in its shape and structure the inherent nature of intuitive mind that is also characterized by coherence.

Intuitive mind can 'look both ways', it draws on the universal and the individual, the inner and the outer. Part of what this means is we have a balanced approach to life: we 'weigh things up'. I sit in the London Science Museum, musing on what I've seen, learning from it and at the same time realizing the discoveries and theories throw up as many questions as they do answers. I am 'open-minded' yet at the same time I am not going to just swallow whole all that I am being told.

But what the experience of intuitive mind also means is that I feel happy. A sense of well-being pervades me and the way I see things. This is because the inherent nature of my inner self *is* well-being. That may be where the phrase comes from because a hidden depth of presence is like a well, fed by underground springs, a sense of something that 'wells' up. We are and we draw on this 'well-being' when we maintain the quality of balanced awareness.

Chapter 2

Template

Two things awe me most, the starry sky above me and the moral law within me.
Immanuel Kant

Temple
That footfall echoing through sacred space
where the carved lineaments are so well placed
and light enamels archways like prayers
lightening between cool stone hands our cares;

we enter, an audience to silence,
uninitiated but taken in
dappled by patterned light, held in balance
our inept casual glance, a kind of sin.

Other places we exist as driven
wind-whipped down the long Manhattan canyons
or past brittle trees arched thinly over
that brown brook lost behind the car dealers –

remember when this temple gets defaced
our bodies are the fractals of its grace.

When we are aware of both the inner and outer self, we feel a sense of well-being and balance. We are also able to think better. This is because we have the resources of our inner presence available to us as well as the input that our senses report to us. And we can draw on intuition, as well as intellect, which is what the phrase 'intuitive mind' implies.

Intuition is about knowing something in a direct way, through immediate apprehension. We sometimes use the phrase 'an intuitive flash' to describe the act of suddenly downloading a solution or a new insight. But although the insight itself is new, and seems to appear in our minds without any prior act of deduction, it is always connected to problems or issues we have been thinking about previously. Einstein, who was a great proponent of the importance of intuition, achieved his insights about relativity after long years of pondering the nature of space and time. Intuitive knowing is also more to do with feeling than logical thought. Einstein said he knew his insights were right, even before he knew why: '... At times I feel certain I am right while not knowing the reason.' So we look at things 'out there' in the dimensional world which our senses report to us, and we think about them, ponder them, analyse them. Then at some point, often when we are engaged in some other way, a solution, a new insight or just the next step crystallizes in our mind. We know it's right, we can feel it. The idea may not come fully formed. We may not know why it is right. But it is. And the proof is in the eating because it works, or it takes us to the next stage of our project. It proves itself to be coherent because it has meaningful and fruitful relationship to the world we live in and the way we live in it.

In simple terms we could say that intuition is thought guided by feeling. But what is it that the feeling connects to? How do we know that our feeling about something as yet somewhat unformed is right, even before we implement it or have a logical reason or proof? Because we are feeling the way this insight connects to our inner self. In his essay on self-reliance, it was this resource of inner direction that Emerson urged his readers to trust and attend to: 'A man should learn to detect and watch that gleam of light which flashes across his mind from within, more than the lustre of the firmament of bards and sages.'

The intuitive flash that lights up is the result of the interrelationship between the two aspects of awareness. As we ponder and think about things with our 'empirical individual' self, we are also getting feedback from the 'universal spiritual' part, and out of this back and forth we spin new solutions.

The word intuition is derived from the Latin *intueri*, which means to look upon, to consider or to contemplate. The derivation of both 'consider' and 'contemplate' have their roots in other Latin words related to the ancient practice of reading the stars for prophetic signs. *Sidera* means stars or constellations; *con* means with. So the literal meaning is 'with the stars'. Contemplate, meanwhile, has the Latin root of *templum* right in the middle of it. *Templum* meant 'an open or consecrated space or sanctuary marked out by the augur for the observation of the sky', which develops the meaning to include the space marked out from which to observe the stars. A sanctuary, a temple, but one with its roof open to the heavens. *Sub specie aeternitatis*, in the presence of the infinity of star-marked space and in the space marked out by the augur: that was the place to go to think deeply, and search out directions for human affairs, based on the signs appearing in the sky.

To consecrate is to set a place apart in which to contemplate deep things, to make sacred. Sacred is similar in meaning to holy and hale, meaning healthy, with no damaged parts, and therefore also to the idea of whole, meaning complete. When intuitive mind emerges in us, our consciousness becomes whole, aware of both inner and outer, the infinite and the finite:

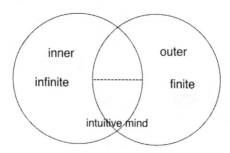

And we are 'open' to the insights that emerge from this relationship. These insights are themselves also 'whole', they replicate its nature. They are sound. Einstein's extraordinary synthesis of insight about the bending of time and space holds up, and leads to a deeper understanding about the universe.

The ancients knew that it was important to act in ways harmonious to the larger whole, so as not to disturb its balance. Nature, the cosmos and human beings were part of a complex web in which every part was meaningfully related and linked. Therefore it was always understood that action must be guided by the process of 'contemplation' so as to allow a whole solution to emerge.

Chapter 3

Opening a Pathway in Thought

Man is all symmetry,
Full of proportions, one limb unto another,
And to all the world besides.
Each part may call the farthest brother,
For head with foot hath private amity,
And both with moons and tides.
from 'Man' by George Herbert

It takes something more than intelligence to act intelligently.
Dostoevsky, *Crime and Punishment*

Contemplation opens a path in thought. The 'Aha' feeling. Often to begin with, it is just that, a path, a sense of where to head. And despite its vagueness, it has the ring of certainty about it. This path does not appear unless the 'temple' of the mind has formed – the awareness poised between inner and outer – which Govinda calls intuitive mind.

The vesica piscis symbol that I use to symbolize the emergence of intuitive mind is created out of the relationship between two circles:

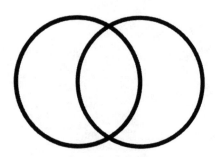

As I have already explored, this symbol embodies the quality of being a unified whole. The third potential forming out of the circles' overlap also symbolizes the way in which a whole is greater than the sum of its parts. The shape is made of two circles, but their relationship creates a new, third potential. It is ready to expand.

Again, as already mentioned, the same symbol also expresses the ancient world's understanding of the principle underlying the emergence of life out of the two orders of heaven and earth. And at least part of the reason such grand significance has accrued to this seemingly simple symbol is due to its function as the root shape of what is generally known as sacred geometry. Once one constructs the two intersecting circles, one can draw a straight line between their centres:

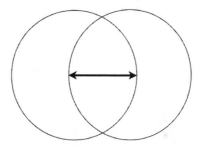

Mathematician Michael Schneider calls this the 'birth of the line'. And from the vesica and the line, all the other shapes of sacred geometry can be constructed:

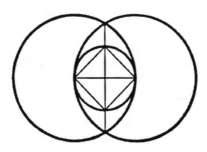

The birth of the line within the vesica piscis is analogous to the path of thought opening in our mind, when we are poised between inner and outer awareness. Just as the further shapes of the triangle and square expand out of the vesica, so further insight will expand out of our intuitive 'lining up'.

The understanding of sacred geometry goes all the way back to Pythagoras (and no doubt beyond) who saw in the mysteries of number and shape a language of harmony and meaningful relationship that was archetypal: underlying, forming and expressed through the myriad shapes of nature, including human beings. Pythagoras wrote nothing down but his work and that of his followers influenced Plato and through him much of the rest of Greek and therefore Western civilization. Others built on his work, discovering that the fundamental shapes generated out of the vesica piscis encode pattern and mathematical formulae that determine the forms and growth cycles of nature.

One spectacular example is the pentagram star (derived from the pentagon and created out of the vesica piscis) whose every part embodies the relationship known as the golden mean or *Phi* (ϕ):

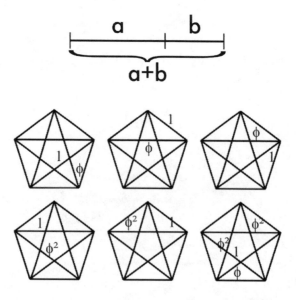

The fractional value of the golden mean or *Phi* is related to the Fibonacci sequence of numbers which describes the genealogy of the honeybee drone, the branching of trees, the average number of petals on flowers and pine needles clustering in different pine species. It also governs the proportions of our faces, our bodies, our arms, legs, hands and feet. Everything is literally clothed in harmony.

When the pathway opens in our thought, we are beginning to create, to spin new perception. The process begins intuitively and becomes more intellectual as it 'grows' and its meaning is extruded. The insights we generate will also be harmonious, because they have formed out of the relationship between our inner self and outer self. Between the infinite and the finite. They will be part of a unified whole.

When asked if he was wise Pythagoras was said to have answered that he was a 'lover of wisdom', thus inventing the term 'philosophy' (*philos* Greek for lover, *sophia* Greek for wisdom). Far from the intellectual analysis of life, which is how we tend to characterize philosophy today, this kind of wisdom had to do with being skilful and of sound judgement, and was something dynamic, active. It meant the ability to work within the ordered cosmos (from a word meaning embroidered i.e. patterned with meaning) in ways that led to effective as well as often beautiful outcomes.

Chapter 4

Unbroken Wholeness

I woke to the exhilarating sense that the unfolding flow of life was not only larger but richer in meaning and interest than my tightly managed model of it had been...
Lindsay Clarke

The Art of Wholeness
Three large oak trees walking down the hill
at sunset, sunrise, through the greys and golds
of days, they edge the meaning of fields
shore up the sky, and slowly let unfold

the valley view. So sublime and easy
so sailing and dark and tall, they never
arrive where they are going, but in their
towering presence all is already

become and everywhere and they are part
of a landscape, and yet they are the art
of wholeness, hologram, roots, branches, life
breaking robustly out of symbol, they are rife

with coherence, leaves, acorns to scatter
then bare to hold the shape of winter.

Like God's finger stretching out across the heavens of the Sistine Chapel's ceiling to meet Adam's, our 'universal spiritual' aspect meets our 'empirical individual' aspect in a grand arc of creation. The products of this meeting, whether they are Michelangelo's magnificent frescoes, Einstein's Theory of Relativity or, on a less grand scale but personal to me, a new poem, will always have the quality of coherence – and originality. In other words, the balanced awareness that Govinda calls 'intuitive mind' is key not only to our wisdom but also to our creativity.

To theoretical physicist David Bohm creativity, whether in scientific thought, art, literature or any other sphere, was essentially the ability to see anew, to let new meaning emerge. And he felt creativity gave evidence of an endless depth of meaning within both matter and human consciousness:

> ...we have to constantly see afresh. For the present we can say that creativity is not only the fresh perception of new meanings, and the ultimate unfoldment of this perception within the manifest and the somatic, but I would say that it is ultimately the action of the infinite in the sphere of the finite – that is, this meaning goes to infinite depths.

There are obvious parallels here with the Buddhist ideas of the infinite depth of 'universal consciousness' which, by means of intuitive mind, acts within the individual finite awareness of space and time:

> [intuitive mind] ... is the principle through which the universal consciousness experiences itself and through which it descends into the multiplicity of things, into the differentiation of senses and sense-objects, out of which arises the experience of the material world.

For Bohm, the encounter with the forces of the subatomic world, that had begun in the early part of the 20th century, required a less linear way of understanding ourselves and the world than had prevailed for so long, as part of our inheritance from Newton's classical or mechanical model of the universe. In his profound analysis of quantum theory, Bohm evolved a radically new approach which involved a deeper order of interiority within the universe itself. In Bohm's theory, the universe is a dynamic system in which aspects unfold into form, and enfold again into what he termed the 'implicate order':

> In terms of the implicate order... one can ascribe the phenomena {i.e. behaviour of sub-atomic particles} to a deeper reality that underlies them...

The implicate order represents an unmanifested condition in which objects are connected in ways that are non-local. Photons of light that can appear either as waves or particles, and particles that appear and disappear in their orbits can be explained in terms of this unfolding and enfolding, which is going on all the time but is 'easier' to detect at the subatomic level:

> We could picture the electron not as a particle that exists continuously but as something coming in and going out and then coming in again. If these various condensations are close together, they approximate a track.

The implicate order is constantly unfolding into the forms and appearances around us. Everything – from the brief glimpse of an electron, to a sunflower, to a human being, to an idea in thought – is unfolded from a deeper order and will be enfolded back into it. Each relatively stable sub-whole of this flowing movement that Bohm called the 'holo-movement' is explicate, and enfolds within it qualities of the larger whole of the implicate order. Therefore, instead of attempting to explain the quantum world in terms that made sense within the classical laws of physics, Bohm turned the matter on its head, and explained the world of space and time in terms of the quantum reality:

> One is led to a new notion of unbroken wholeness which denies

the classical idea of analyzability of the world into separately existing parts… We have reversed the usual classical notion that the independent 'elementary parts' of the world are the fundamental reality, and that the various systems are merely particular contingent forms and arrangements of these parts. Rather, we say that inseparable quantum interconnectedness of the whole universe is the fundamental reality, and that relatively independent behaving parts are merely particular and contingent forms within this whole.

In this view of things, the implicate order is shaped and changed by the expansion of itself by means of the sub-wholes, or parts, or aspects of the explicate order; and likewise the explicate is expanded and altered by the evolving possibilities engendered in the implicate. In both directions, from the explicate into the implicate and vice versa, meaning can be continuously extended:

What this implies is that meaning is capable of an indefinite extension to ever greater levels of subtlety as well as of comprehensiveness –

What is explicate helps to engender new starting points that are incubated within the implicate; what is stored as possibility in the implicate is the shaping blueprint for new forms in the explicate. Bohm speculated that this movement between the implicate and explicate order may be the deeper mechanism involved in the processes of evolution.

Bohm's ideas give us a holistic view of the universe and our place within it that also reprieves ancient insights about an ordered and interwoven cosmos in which human beings had a significant part to play. We participate in this dynamic and evolving universe through our creativity. We ourselves expand meaning by reason of the relationship between our inner and outer self:

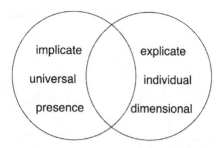

Through our interaction with the explicate, at all levels – the physical world, other people, ideas, thoughts – we are continually challenged to expand our experience: figure out why photons of light are behaving the way they do, paint a painting with a style or form that has never existed before, or build a car engine that cuts down pollution by using less gas. And as we *contemplate* our intimations and aims, the implicate level forms into new patterns of meaning, some in the form of intuitive flashes, others in the gradual emergence into awareness of the next steps to take. These then feed back into the explicate as ideas and actions and eventually finished projects. The movement between the implicate and the explicate in our perceptual process is how we participate in a profound and meaningful relationship with the universe of unbroken wholeness.

Chapter 5

The Measure of Self

Man, know thyself in true proportion.
Oracle of Delphi

Crossing over and back and finding the balance
or just stepping out again is a freedom so
light it needs no marking, so profound, its trophy
can only be awarded me myself, worn like
a piece of artisan jewelry, bought by myself
for me, hanging in the centre through the window
of the thymus, glowing like a rainbow bridging
gold, the one world turning back into the other.
from 'The Labyrinth'

According to Bohm's understanding, the manifested world exists in relationship with a deeper order, that is non-manifest. The one emerges from the other, and folds back into it and this interaction between what he termed the explicate and the implicate orders develops and extends the meaning of both. Our consciousness is designed to participate in this same expansion of meaning out of the interchange of the inner and outer. The *Mahayana-Sraddhotpada-Sastra* says that intuitive mind: 'has two doors from which issue its activities'. When we function in the balanced awareness of intuitive mind, with both 'doors' open, one to the inner implicate order, one to the outer, explicate realm, our thinking becomes generative.

The 'two doors' of intuitive mind could be likened to the two primary ways we perceive and think. Feeling and thought, heart and mind. Using the shape of the vesica again as an analogy for consciousness, we could call one of the circles' centres heart, and the other mind:

23

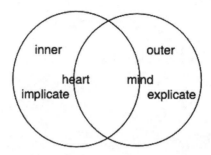

The heart is 'closer' to the inner realm, because it is primarily through feeling that we perceive this realm; the mind is 'closer' to the outer, because its job is dominantly to collect data and input from the outer. The heart is drawing on the inner and the implicate; the mind is drawing on the outer and the explicate. We could think of them as two radiating centres of awareness whose energies overlap to form the field of our consciousness:

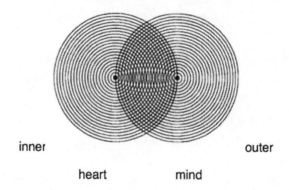

Returning again to the geometric properties of the vesica piscis, mathematician Michael Schneider explains that if we draw the vesica piscis with these multiple concentric rings the lattice created by the circles overlapping: 'establish(es) the precise mathematical distances and relationships required to construct the basic geometric shapes and patterns that recur through the universe.'

But this lattice only forms when the circumference of each circle intersects the other's centre. In other words, unless this happens there will be a partial overlapping pattern created, yet not the full complexity: 'When the distance between centers is one (unit) then the relationships reveal themselves.' Moreover, it is only when the two centres are intersected, that the straight line between them can be drawn.

In terms of our consciousness, the lining up of the two centres symbolizes well those flashes of intuitive insight when we suddenly get the next step to take, or a solution to a problem. Heart and mind, inner and outer awareness, line up in a new way. It is as if they find themselves in a new realization, which is also a new *relationship*. Their 'centres' align. Alignment means literally a-line-ment. A straight line.

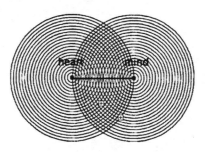

The path opening in thought. This lining up is always very noticeable. We do not have to question it, only let it continue to expand because implicit in its emergence is the 'lattice' of new possibility that is being evolved out of the interaction between the implicate and explicate orders.

I call this lining up in ourselves the fundamental relationship of meaning. It is the insight that has emerged out of balanced awareness, and which therefore fits. Whether it leads to the right words, or brushstroke, or other action. This sense of finding the right meaning for ourselves is an interior act. We arrive at it from within ourselves.

The way to go is not always clear. We often have to ponder our aims and dilemmas for a while, to let the sense of direction emerge.

But when it does it will always feel balanced and 'measured'. To quote David Bohm again: 'measure is a form of insight that has to fit the overall reality in which man lives, as demonstrated by the clarity of perception and harmony of action to which it leads.'

Finding the interior alignment could also be called finding the measure of ourself. 'This above all, to thine own self be true' is the advice Polonius gives to his son in Shakespeare's *Hamlet*. Stay true, stay aligned with your own sense of direction. Don't be unduly influenced by others' opinions, or talked out of your own intimations. We have this sense that the real measure of a person is their integrity, their ability to be 'true' – not rigid or myopic – but true to the direction of their own unfoldment.

Chapter 6

The Owl Appears

As soon as thought comes
out of the trees directly ahead
and slightly below
a sudden whir
of wings
the barred uniform
patterns on soft brown body
and wing span
perfect round head
staring darkness
of an owl
flying up the sloping path
towards us,
over our heads
and turning
its back now
flapping off down
the grey corridor of pines.

An owl at mid-day
summoned from its sleep
by the still intent
of my meditations,
Merlin's familiar
an answering sign
out of the forest itself.
from 'The Prayer & the Creation'

Depending on what we are focussing upon, the lining up of heart and mind will feel more or less intense. My decision, for instance, to phone my friend and meet for coffee involves a fairly relaxed level of energy. Meeting up might make us want to get together more regularly, a thought that has a greater energy to it. In all this activity, meaning is being exchanged and expanded between the implicate and explicate levels. The idea of having coffee with my friend is implicate to phoning her up and meeting. My action of having coffee is explicate to the thought it engenders of meeting regularly. But if suddenly, sitting there in conversation, something about the light through the window, the trees in the square outside, catalyses perception, snatches of words, and the beginning of a poem occurs to me, then the whole interaction has become explicate to a still more intense level of energy and meaning from the implicate. There is a qualitative difference between the impulse to call my friend, and the inspiration that conjures the poem. The former is like a quick flash, which, if I follow up on it, often has a synchronicity that makes things work out easily. But the latter emerges from a deeper place.

David Bohm realized there were different levels in the implicate order: 'If I see an implicate becoming explicate, then I think of a still deeper implicate from which arose the force which made it move from the implicate to the explicate... And I am suggesting that these processes have access to an, in principle, unlimited depth in the implicate order.'

Our creativity gives evidence of an infinite depth of meaning within the implicate order. This is because our inner self goes to infinite depths. There is no end to us, in this sense. But the implicate order does not only apply to human consciousness. All of matter is intricately linked in to the implicate: it is the explicate, manifest form of one unbroken universe, temporarily displaying for us aspects of itself. Matter also has no end to it. In fact, according to Bohm, this is the fundamental implication of quantum theory – there is no ultimate material building block to be found: 'It is not commonly realized... that the quantum theory implies that no such bottom level of unambiguous reality is possible.'

This in turn has implications for the relationship between matter and our own consciousness. And once again the ancient symbol of the vesica piscis can help us think some of this through.

We have seen that as a geometric construction, if we draw the vesica with concentric circles, a lattice or a matrix forms that establishes the mathematical relationships generating the basic shapes and patterns that recur through the cosmos:

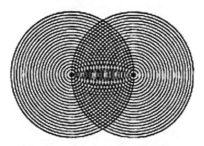

Additionally, in folklore and mythic archetype, the shape created by the overlap of the two circles is associated with the vulva of the mother goddess, out of whom all the forms of life are birthed. This association is due both to the geometric attributes of the vesica and to its shape. The pagan figures of the Sheela-na-gigs found carved on old churches, for instance, hold open their perfectly symmetrical vulva with their hands:

The Sanskrit word for vulva is yoni, and also connotes a source and an originating matrix. Added to this are further associations from the ancient Egyptian hieroglyph in the shape of a mouth, that both means mouth and has the phonetic sound of R, linking to words like Ra, Re or Ru, which denote the creator, or the forces of the creator. As if this shape is the mouth through which the creator expresses. Both layerings of meaning are at work when we see the carving of Christ in the mandorla (almond) shape on the facade of Chartres Cathedral!

In all three examples – the vulva of the mother goddess, the mouth of the creator and Christ in the mandorla – the vesica shape symbolizes a portal out of which the powers of the creator emerge.

Our consciousness, when intuitive mind is in place, is that matrix, that portal out of which the forms of life – our insights and ideas – appear, which are themselves generative: they will be fruitful. Moreover, the energy that expresses through this matrix is our deeper identity, the creator identity. That which goes to infinite depths.

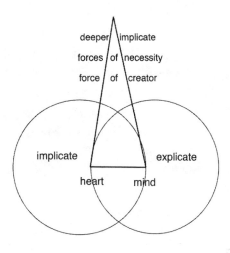

Through the radiating centres of heart and mind, the implicate meshes into the explicate, and vice versa. But in both domains, awareness goes to infinite depths. Our inner self connects us to a force that wells up through the whole field of awareness, and 'speaks' through that 'mouth': 'And God *said*, "Let there be light", God here denoting the potent level of creator energy that stirs the pot of matter at deep levels, shaping it into matching manifestation: 'and there was light.'

The deeper the revelation of meaning from the implicate, the more deeply we see into the meaning of the explicate; and vice versa. We can 'see the world in a grain of sand'. We also find that the world of form begins to participate in our thought process, as correlates shape around us to reflect the new meaning. If Einstein was stymied in his thought process, he would sit down at the piano, play for a while, then say, 'I have it now,' meaning the next step in his understanding. The music acted as a non-logical correlate that helped shape previously unformed insight. When Archimedes (of 3rd century Greece) supposedly sat down in his bath and yelled out, '*Eureka*,' meaning (similarly), 'I've found it,' he meant the solution to a difficult problem had just been suggested to him by the displacement of water caused by his body. What he saw suddenly was that by submerging in water the golden crown of Hiero of Syracuse he could measure its volume. Hiero was worried his goldsmith had cheated him by substituting silver. The ratio of the crown's volume to its weight would give density – a good indicator of purity. In this example, the act of sitting in the bath prompted the idea of submerging the crown.

Once while walking through the Cotswold Hills in England and meditating on two different chains of thought, I found the landscape turning into a correlate of my thought process. As I headed down one of the small rolling hills, the left side of the path gave a view out over distant fields, the other was bordered by dark pine woods. I had been pondering the symbolic meaning of Merlin's fate, trapped in his crystal cave, while at the same time wondering why the local people seemed so downtrodden, even though they lived in such a beautiful place. Walking and looking around, I suddenly realized that the two thought processes answered each other – Merlin represented the creative power in ourselves that we seem cut off from when we feel trapped in our circumstances. The two chains of thought were the same, just as the two views linked to the same path I was walking down. At the very moment of my realization, a large brown and cream barred owl came flying up the path toward me, turned over my head and flew into the pine trees. It was noon, and the owl should really have been fast asleep, but it seemed to have been summoned by my thoughts as Merlin's familiar, confirming my insight.

The experience of our thought shaping and corresponding with elements of the natural world lies behind the ritual of the Native American vision quest, when a young man went out into the wilderness to fast and survive on his own. During this time, a creature would often appear, as an embodiment of his own spirit and purpose and to signal the end of his quest. Jung has this to say about the connection between the world of form and our consciousness: 'Since psyche and matter are contained in one and the same world and moreover are in continuous contact with one another and ultimately rest on irrepresentable, transcendent factors, it is not only possible but fairly probable, even, that psyche and matter are two different aspects of one and the same thing.'

The creative power of consciousness when intuitive mind is in place has more often been called in the West the power of the imagination. Coleridge called the imagination a 'shaping spirit' that 'balances and fuses the innate capacities and powers of the mind with the external presence of the objective world that the mind receives through the senses.' Novelist Lindsay Clarke feels that as humans: 'we are all filaments of the planet's living intelligence and that, if we only open our senses clearly enough to listen, it speaks to us through the active imagination in the language of the soul.' Philosopher and writer Richard Tarnas in his book *The Passion of the Western Mind* writes: 'Nature becomes intelligible to itself through the human mind... And it is only when the human mind actively brings forth from within itself the full powers of a disciplined imagination and saturates its empirical observation with archetypal insight that the deeper reality of the world emerges.' There is a sense of magic about this, and the root 'ma' in the word imagination links to the word magic, and the Sanskrit *ma* meaning create, and thus *maya* which means the power by which the universe becomes manifest, or matter. In what Bohm called the activity of meaning, he came to see mind and matter as two aspects of one process, rather like a magnet that has two poles, which are nevertheless not actually separate, but two aspects of one flowing system.

Chapter 7

Seamless

Beauty then is a relation.
Gerard Manley Hopkins

Art
If you find that luminous blue bubble
whose irregular roundness can wobble
and squeeze between things yet still hold its shape
it will roll over your affairs and escape
like an eye, a fluid lens, a droplet
that magnifies with no fixed comment yet
on its curved distorted focus. It must
be made well, constructed out of itself
in such a way that it has no edges
no unravelling seams but is endless
and flares up translucent like a blue flame
answering with the wholeness of its name.

The seamless relationship between matter and meaning is what gives art – whether in the form of paintings and sculpture, music, literature or great architecture – its unique hallmark. When an artist is able to fashion forms out of the relationship of inner and outer awareness, he or she is able to produce work that lasts.

The creative process often begins with an unfocussed observation of something 'out there': something someone said, an impression of place, the echoes of tradition. In my example of sitting in a cafe, it is the ambience, the trees, the light, that catalyse an impulse. If I focus on it, this impulse intensifies into something more definite: the line between heart and mind begins to form. Looking again at the vesica with concentric circles as a symbol of consciousness, when heart and mind line up, in addition to the lattice, there is a row of seed-like shapes that form along the line between the two centres:

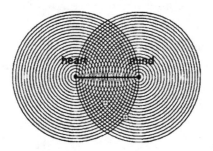

These seed shapes symbolize well for me the bubbling up of intimations and essences of mood or theme which accompany the emergence of an artistic intention:

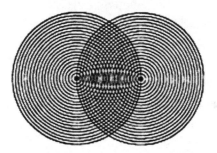

These pre-form possibilities are like code that is not yet understood. They will have to be translated gradually, guided by the feedback of our feeling perception from the inner. Depending on the medium, the code will turn into colours, shapes, musical phrases, word phrases, sketches, drafts. The musical phrase gets expanded into a symphony, the word phrase becomes a poem, the theme informs a novel, the sketches turn into a painting or sculpture or building. The process is exponential, because the more the form emerges, the more it feeds back into the intention to help the process of embodiment.

Bit by bit the straw of our unworked experience and impressions are spun into the gold of art. The visit of Napoleon is turned into the *Eroica* symphony; the wind-beaten shapes of Cornwall's West Penwith into sculpture; the demands of royal propaganda into history plays. What is created is an artefact, something fashioned out of the relationship between inner and outer awareness, not constructed from an intellectual measuring tape. Like a hologram, each part embodies the shape or theme of the whole: in each musical period we hear a differentiation of the symphony; in each chunk of iambic pentameters we hear echoes of the play; in each word of the poem we see through a facet into its voice and theme. Moreover, each part unfolds with a kind of inevitability, as if its sequence is also determined by the intention of the whole, the way a path must wind this way and that to accommodate the valley's shape on its way to the sea. In visual arts, this hologram-like quality is more to do with the inherent indivisibility of the piece. This quality of 'unbroken wholeness' is what differentiates visual art from decoration, literature from well-crafted journalism.

A work of art forms a whole that is more than the sum of its parts and which therefore cannot be understood by reducing it to its parts. This whole thing that now exists, that did not exist before, is what makes art transformative, and is the mystery that intellect alone cannot bring about. Without access to the deep implicate, we will be more likely to repeat what already exists; to write plays that display the current politically correct way of thinking about ourselves and society; make films that cover up their paucity of theme with an overdose of special effects, or violence or cringingly unerotic sex, or a mixture of all three; or line up a few bricks on the floor and write a two-page account of their unintelligible meaning.

Art can be transformative because it helps us see new meaning ourselves. In the curved, hollowed stone or wooden forms of Barbara Hepworth's sculptures, strung with wire or string, both at rest and in motion, we see echoes of the landscape where she lived: the rounded, weather-beaten moors of Cornwall's farthest tip, threaded with telephone wires, and stacked with Neolithic dolmen. We also see the synthesis between Hepworth's outer awareness and her inner aims as an artist. The sculptures embody this relationship. A work of art has a meaning that is inherent because it is a product of, a result of, the relationship between inner and outer. It holds this meaning for us, and when we interact with it, we can be drawn back into awareness of our own depth of field. Visionary architect Christopher Alexander writes about the power of art to do this:

> the ultimate questions of architecture and art concern some connection of incalculable depth, between made work (building, painting, ornament, street) and the inner 'I' which each of us experiences. What I call 'the I' is that interior element in a work of art, which makes one feel related to it. It may occur in a leaf, or in a picture, in a house, in a wave, even in a grain of sand, or in an ornament. It is not ego. It is not me. It is not individual at all, having to do with me, or you. It is humble, and enormous: that thing in common which each one of us has in us…
> For I believe… that the thing I call the I, which lives at the core of our experience, is a real thing, existing in all matter, beyond ourselves, and that we must understand it this way in order to make sense of living structure, of buildings, of art, and of our place in the world.

The interior element in art which Alexander calls the 'I' is the quality of internal relatedness which the work of art displays for us and which resonates with our own nature. The same quality, as he also acknowledges in this passage, is found in the natural world. When a form displays this relationship to us, it also displays what beauty is. Beauty is difficult to define because its attributes are part dimensional, part undimensional. Part form, part mystery. While some of the influences that shape a work of art can be traced from circumstances or tradition, ultimately its form is seamless because it was generated out of the interaction between awareness of what already existed and what was forming in the implicate of new meaning. We cannot see exactly how it was made because it trails off into the invisible. Beauty, as Gerard Manley Hopkins wrote, 'is a relation'. A relationship not only of the parts to one another, and to the whole structure; but also a relation of the form to the inspired, the not-seen-before insight. In fact, an embodiment of this new relationship. This quality of relatedness in the form itself, and the feeling it engenders within us, are both beautiful – full of beauty, wonder, awe. And this experience of shared beauty, both apprehended and engendered, renews and nourishes our psyche.

Chapter 8

Love & Meaningful Relationship

And love is something eternal, it may change in aspect but not in essence.

Vincent van Gogh

– whatever can impart
a benediction, the only way we ever
build what we love, when this spills easily over
and that space out there, those hills, the tower and town
square, become the place that matches, catches and turns
back through us its meaning, like sunlight on canyon
walls, like faces we can see clear through to the sun.

from 'See Clear Through to the Sun'

We cannot define the inner self intellectually, but we can feel it. We feel the sense of well-being, or we feel joyful, buoyant. This level of ourselves is characterized by general qualities whose intensity and nature varies. At its most intense, we know it as love. Love is the deeper identity, the force that goes to infinite depth and which resonates with the deep mystery of 'I' in the realm of form as perceived by our senses. When this level of ourself is engaged, we will only be able to produce outcomes that are in accordance with us – ideas that are sound, art that is beautiful. And we will only act toward others in ways that are kindly.

Scientists who explain human beings on the basis of genetics and cultural background alone have sometimes found the existence of love puzzling. Love for one's mate or one's children can be explained as a form of self-interest, an extension of our survival instincts, but those occasions when people act from selfless love and altruism seem inexplicable. If, however, love is understood as the fundamental nature of our inner presence, these actions are no longer anomalies but instances of this deeper nature acting in ways that are characteristic of itself. Our personality self takes on the nature of our inner self when we know love. Moreover, when we know love, we are active, we are lov-ing. The love doesn't just stay inside us, it spills over, and the people and things that enter our conscious awareness – whether in thought, or as part of our physical circumstances – are held in love and seen as meaning-fully related to us. In fact love is perhaps best understood as the experience of meaningful relationship, both experienced within ourselves and extended to others.

Love as an experience of meaningful relationship is different from the *attempt* to love someone (or everyone). It is not the attempt to gush loving emotion over others indiscriminately. It involves compassion, but also measure and proportion. A simple example is my experience one spring when I had cut back two overgrown evergreen trees that act as a hedge between our property and our neighbour's. In the new sparseness of the pruned trees, I could see that my neighbour had encroached on our property. He had placed a bin of leaf mulch on it, he'd leant some old fencing on our side of the fence and dumped ash there from his fire. At first I felt resentful and thought about retaliatory action. I'd shove the stuff back on to his property, or send a slightly cool email. But then I recalled all the things he has done for us over many years; how we have worked together on garden projects that have benefited both of us, how we are friends. I knew my first thoughts were reactive, and did not fit the overall context of our relationship. And I re-evaluated what to do. In the end, I did ask him to move his things, but in a non-confrontational way, explaining that I was going to store the garden bins there, and he offered to cut down a couple of the thicker branches of the evergreens with his chainsaw. He also told me of his longer-term plans for building a proper storage area, and strengthening the existing fence. And I saw that he had simply grown forgetful about what he was doing, or was seeing it in the context of his future plans. So the situation worked out creatively, and I could feel as soon as my thoughts changed that they were more in tune with my deeper self. In my initial reaction, I was playing out a recognizable aspect of an 'individual empirical' consciousness. Someone whose irritation at her untidy garden caused by her neighbour started to turn her into a slightly sour nag. But then as I weighed things up, more of the 'universal' part showed up. I took a larger view of things, my actions grew out of this larger view and the situation resolved.

The sense of expanded identity frees us up, and gives us traction in relating to others. Secure in our own worthiness, we are less reactive, and better able to communicate cleanly about potentially tricky situations. We are also less likely to view others as the source of either our happiness or our problems. This is particularly helpful in our intimate partnerships, because often the very closeness of these relationships can convince us that our source of well-being lies in the other person, instead of in ourselves, causing us to focus outwardly on them. If this shift happens, it becomes very easy to feel that one's quality and circumstances of life are at the mercy of or dictated by the other. Whether it be our joy or our discontent that we pin on them. The result can be either a sense of insecurity and dependency, or the feeling of being trapped and irritated. Knowing that our primary fulfilment is found in relationship with our inner self removes this belief, with its unconscious demand, and makes everything more spacious and enjoyable. The same spaciousness is possible in our relationships generally – we find it easier to accept other people without having to judge them or need them to think and act the way we want them to. In fact, we are much more open to listening to what others have to say, and to learn from their experience and perspective.

Essentially, when we connect to the flow of love at the core of ourselves, we realize that the same flow moves within all people, and that we share an implicit commonality with every other person. This means that we know what is fundamentally true of others, and therefore are able to relate to the whole of them, not just the 'parts' of their individual personality. And this approach makes the differences – of background, beliefs and goals – easier to navigate.

Once my sense of identity expanded, I related to my neighbour in parallel ways. In other words, instead of viewing him as only the 'individual empirical' bit, someone who had encroached on my property without telling me, I remembered the 'universal spiritual' part as well – the person who loans us tools, lends us his truck, gives us samples of the bread he makes. I related to the whole of him, not the part of him, and that made all the difference.

Rooted in the general and common realm of being, we feel more relaxed about the specific individual differences of personality and competing aims: why my neighbour put his leaf bin on my side of the fence. At the same time, we will tend to draw out the best in others because we will focus naturally on the attitudes in them that resonate with their own inner self as opposed to those which hold them in discord. I remember the way my neighbour helps us. I talk to him about the encroachment, and he moves the bin, and helps cut back more of my overgrown shrubs! Knowing that we already share common ground in the realm of being makes it easier to arrive at common ground – often literally – in the world of space and time.

Chapter 9

The Path Through the Maze

Show not what has been done, but what can be. How beautiful the world would be if there were a procedure for moving through labyrinths.

Umberto Eco, *The Name of the Rose*

Thin Places
*Each morning what is familiar is seen
again, as we awaken out of night
and our part of Earth spins round into light –
that day-shift still traveling while they dream.*

*Continents, neighbourhoods striped in darkness
and sun light, oceans tilted warm then cold –
it is this interchange that grows the world,
makes the soft grey overlap that stretches*

*out the dusk, the mist that blurs the morning
land. Thin places, the Celts said, where the deep
bleeds through and shifts the hardened shape of things,
a clearing like the night that mimics sleep.*

*This is the world riddle that we answer
when we see one depth within the other.*

The whole self is the coherent self, and the foundation of coherence in our lives. Generative insight and outcome, creativity and meaningful relationship with others are all facilitated by the whole identity functioning through the balanced awareness of intuitive mind. However, this balance is only possible while we maintain awareness of the inner self. In this sense there is a hierarchy to our consciousness. Without the infinite depth of the 'universal spiritual' there is nothing against which to measure the finite of our 'individual empirical' experience. If the mind spins in circles without reference to the forming pattern of the implicate, the measure of self, the sense of alignment between mind and heart, cannot appear:

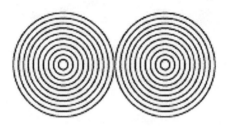

Therefore, it becomes more difficult to 'make meaning' from our circumstances, or find the path through them.

It has become deeply counter-intuitive for us to think this way, to lean in to the invisible potential inside us. We are much more used to guiding our actions by intellectually weighing up the pros and cons, or looking at precedent, or listening to what others think we should do or want us to do. But as a result, we often end up lost in the maze of circumstance.

In Greek myth, Theseus was able to find his way through the maze of Knossos by following Ariadne's thread. The thread symbolizes the steps we take that are the right ones because we are guided by the relationship between inner and outer awareness. Without Ariadne's thread, Theseus would have become confused and lost and been eaten by the Minotaur.

We ourselves must bring the access to the inner pattern in order to complete the picture of what we see. If we try to figure out what to do based solely on analysing what already exists, we will not arrive at a clear sense of direction.

Some intriguing parallels to these ideas are found in Aboriginal customs from the remote Vanuatu Island of Malekula. The Malekulans believed in an afterlife that was attained through a strange series of rites during their present life. Part of these rites involved learning by drawing on the ground complicated geometric but symmetrical maze-like patterns called Nahals:

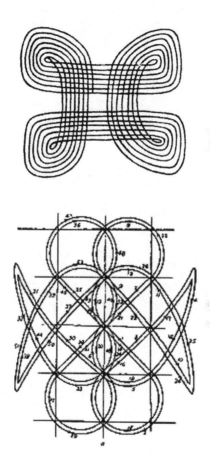

Examples of Malekulan Nahals

When a person died, the belief was that their spirit passed along a road towards the land of the dead. Partway along, their spirit would meet a female guardian ghost sitting on a rock. In front of her on the ground would be drawn a complete version of one of the Nahals they had learned. The path that the dead person's spirit must take lies down the middle of this shape, between its two halves. But as their spirit approaches, the guardian hurriedly rubs out one half of the Nahal pattern. If the spirit knows the Nahal figure, he immediately completes the half which the ghost rubbed out, and passes down the track in the middle of the shape. But if not, he can no longer find the way, and starts to wander about, confused. Only knowledge of the Nahal's pattern can free the spirit from this impasse. Otherwise the ghost, knowing the spirit will never reach the land of the dead and the afterlife, eats him.

The two halves of the Nahal pattern recall the symbol of the vesica piscis with radiating circles. Their intermeshing reveals the path down the middle, the direction to take when inner and outer, heart and mind, line up.

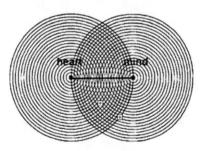

If one of the circles is 'rubbed out', the line between them cannot form: we cannot 'think straight'. Therefore in order to find the way through, one must remember the whole pattern and join the two halves up in awareness.

It's curious that in both the Greek myth and the Malekulan beliefs, the protagonist, if he cannot find his way through the maze, will become lost and then eaten up! It is a graphic way of depicting how we become 'entangled' in problems and dilemmas, or 'devoured' by the pressures around us.

Ariadne's thread turned the Knossos maze into a labyrinth. A maze has lots of false trails and dead ends. A labyrinth has only one path in and out. The ancient art of labyrinth walking is a ritual meditation which aids us in the evolution of new meaning through the meshing of inner and outer awareness. On the way in, we reflect on a question or issue, at the centre we pause to come into balance and into the present moment, and then walk back, retracing the same path. During the walk out, the answer will often come to mind.

When we allow the measure of self to form inside ourselves, the maze of our circumstances is turned into a labyrinth. Instead of pursuing ideas or directions that lead nowhere we participate in the continuous expansion of insight and ideas that fit in harmonious ways within our lives.

Chapter 10

The Hierarchy of our Brain

Cut into rough green turf,
remembered with stone dust,
weeding, the pilgrims turn
and wind the grooved pathways
like glockenspiel

laid down in the underworld
of myth, hidden ground plan
of a citadel we still puzzle through
following its thread into and back
and then

because the reflection
is born on the wings of light-speed –
back again

out of the silence of sight
each pixel of infinity
sent for cataloguing on the left
to feed back to the right
the map we need to manage
the panoramic sweep of what
we are
from 'The Labyrinth'

Walking the labyrinth may be a ritual enactment of a process that goes on in our brain. In fact, the human brain looks a bit like a labyrinth, with its two interconnected halves, forming a roughly circular shape:

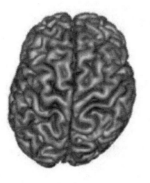

The brain functions as one system, with both hemispheres involved in every activity, yet the two hemispheres are deeply divided, with only a relatively narrow connection via the cerebral cortex. According to psychiatrist and author Iain McGilchrist the reason for this division is that each hemisphere attends to the world very differently. The right brain maintains a broad open awareness of everything, it recognizes what is new, understands what is implicit. The left brain is able to focus narrowly and exactly, is more logical and prefers what is predictable. When we think about something, we 'walk' through both halves, as it were, drawing on both processes to arrive at a solution.

The left brain is more at home in the explicate world, in what has already formed, already happened, and with assessment of immediate circumstances; while the right brain is more at home in the implicate, it is comfortable with the idea that there are potentials and realities we cannot understand intellectually and better at perceiving what is emergent. This makes me think of the Greek god Janus who had two faces: one looked back at the past, one forward into the future. To come up with fresh ideas that work, we need to do both. In this way the brain seems designed to help us continue to grow meaning and expand the world we live in by means of the interaction between the two halves of itself.

Both hemispheres are essential, yet in his book *The Master and his Emissary: The Divided Brain and the Making of the Western World* ultimately McGilchrist argues for the primacy of the right brain, because without its ability to see widely and deeply and to register new possibility, life becomes mechanical and lacks meaning. McGilchrist concludes that the brain's structure may be related to the fundamental nature of the universe itself: 'I believe our brains… are likely themselves to reflect, in their structure and functioning, the nature of the universe in which they have come about.'

The structure of the brain appears to be a duality, in which two complementary aspects interact to create a whole interpretation of experience. A similar principle is at work in the dualities of identity and awareness. Inner and personality self, intuition and intellect. Both aspects of awareness are needed to create new insight, but the process is anchored in the expansiveness of the inner.

Walking the labyrinth – moving between inner and outer awareness, engaging with the two hemispheres of the brain – allows us to evolve insight that is informed by both the realities of circumstance, and the larger possibilities of the forming implicate. The reference to the larger domain of the implicate is essential to growth and coherence. Without it, we are likely to become entrenched in the same old ways of thinking and doing things.

Chapter 11

How We Malfunction

Will not a tiny speck very close to our vision blot out the glory of the world, and leave only a margin by which we see the blot? I know no speck so troublesome as self.
George Eliot, *Middlemarch*

At this threshold
all grows cathedral vast
and very small
there is no scale,
only sheerness
easily blurred,
where the weave can falter, alter itself
from 'Light Way'

The 'universal spiritual' is not more important than the 'individual empirical'. They are partners in creation. But without awareness of the inner, our consciousness malfunctions.

In other words, if the door to the inner gets slammed shut, and only the other door is left open, the awareness of our individual empirical self is all that is left. Our interior sense of space diminishes, along with our sense of well-being. At the same time, without the balancing influence of that deeper part, circumstances around us come to dominate our awareness, almost as if they seep into us, or take us over. And often, due to the shift in our internal assurance, they can seem overwhelming or bleak. Instead of sitting in enjoyment and reflection in the Science Museum, I begin to feel tired by the noise of so many people, and by more information than I can assimilate, and maybe a little depressed at the exhibit's implications that we human beings are predictable, like lab rats in a complex experiment. I think about the journey home and how crowded with more lab rats the Tube will be, and start wishing I'd never come.

What is starting to happen here is that my whole identity is being replaced with a partial sense of identity which in turn affects the way I perceive the world around me.

In Hans Christian Andersen's story *The Snow Queen*, the little boy Kai gets a splinter of the troll mirror lodged in his heart. The mirror fragment distorts reality, making what was beautiful seem ugly. When we lose our connection to the inner, it is like having a splinter of this same distorting mirror lodged in our heart. We feel fractured and disgruntled and our attitude to others and the world around is coloured by these negative feelings.

The way our consciousness works is therefore intimately bound up with our sense of identity and vice versa. Intuitive mind while it remains attuned to the inner self allows this deeper aspect to be known and in relationship with the outer. Our identity partakes of both aspects. We have a personality self, coloured and shaped by DNA, background, culture, and we also draw on the inner self or 'universal consciousness' whose deepest nature is love. We live in both worlds: we participate directly in a quality that goes to infinite depths, as well as in the unique facets of our peculiar human selves. So we have an expanded sense of ourselves, we feel whole, we live in a large place.

However, if we lose our attunement to the inner, not only can we start to feel diminished and controlled by our circumstances, we then go one stage further and make things even worse, by setting out to compensate for these uncomfortable experiences. And our attempts to make up for the interior disconnect end up entrenching the problem.

Once again the Buddhist cosmology of the subtleties of consciousness supplies a graphic depiction of this process. According to Govinda, the partial sense of self that arises when we lose awareness of the inner can become mistaken for the whole self or for the 'real and permanent center of [the] personality'. It is not the whole self, but it thinks it is. Govinda calls this condition 'defiled mind'. One of the propensities of 'defiled mind' is an over-reliance on intellectual analysis of the 'outer'. This tendency is of course inevitable given the fact that the intuitive, heart-centred awareness is now decreased:

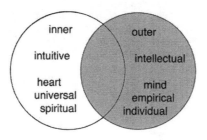

Emergence of 'defiled mind' and dominance of the intellect.

The mind or intellect is more focussed to begin with on the phenomenal world, and as awareness of the inner fades, the intellect steps up its efforts to figure things out by analysis of what already exists.

The Buddhists distinguish the intellect from intuitive mind, essentially correlating their two functions with what I am calling mind and heart. 'Intellectual mind' is the aspect of intelligence that thinks analytically and logically, and divides the world into parts: it sorts, categorizes and discriminates. Clearly we need this aspect of mind, and there is nothing wrong with it when the 'door' to the 'universal consciousness' is kept open, and intuitive mind is functioning in balance. This is why Einstein said that 'the intuitive mind is a sacred gift, the rational mind is a faithful servant.' He meant that the rational or intellectual aspect of mind is there to serve the intuitive mind, by inputting data from the world around. But intellectual analysis that does not take into account the deeper order of meaning can become incoherent because the 'line of measure' cannot form between heart and mind (or intuitive mind and intellectual mind). And therefore the full architecture of thought does not emerge which would allow us to synthesize the ideas that work, or the ways to create great art, or know what the right direction is for us. As a result our ideas and our creations will be 'half-baked'. Flawed. More of the same. Essentially, we can no longer think in 'whole' ways. We think in partial ways.

Chapter 12

Inflation

Psychologically we are all broken up, and with these fragments of ourselves we look at life. And then we say, 'Intellectually I understand, but I cannot act.' So, mental examination or exploration is fragmentary, superficial, and it does not bring about understanding.
J. Krishnamurti

Structural Trap
What's precious, powerful is trapped, headache
for the oil industry, analogy
for its consultants, speciality
of those whose interests are not at stake.

Frame it, don't confront: avoidance tactic –
gagged by the layout, even to be there
is to agree. Intrigue so ironic –
smart, sharp structures obscuring what is clear,

selling out the very depth that could free
us. Thirty pieces, small ball usury
the real thing bartered, exchanged for less,
safe-bet surface value – high-cost success:

some things have so much worth they fetch no price,
never confuse power with compromise.

When 'defiled mind' takes over, and believes it is now the 'real and permanent' centre of the personality, it has lost the relationship with the largeness of the inner self. The sense of being part of something expansive and whole has been replaced by a sense of diminishment which then leads to fear. To make up for this, the diminished identity promptly inflates and thinks of itself as if it *is* the whole thing. This means that the intellect begins to be informed by the substitute self, and, increasingly under the thrall of involvement with what already exists (the 'outer'), becomes endlessly dissecting and dissatisfied seeking to control or manipulate conditions to satisfy the inflation. Without the overarching context of wholeness, its activity leads to what the Buddhists call 'error': 'It is because of the activities of the discriminating-mind that error arises.' (Quoted from the *Lankavatara Sutra*).

For this is when the intellect's activity can run away with itself. A contemporary example was the Wall Street investment banks' 'securitized assets' madness that caused the 2008 crash. These were the complex investment packages that were mixed together with toxic mortgages, given triple 'A' ratings, and sold to clients worldwide. The intellect fused with the partial but inflated identity dissects the whole into meaningless fragments in order to aggrandize itself. Fragments are not the same as parts. A part has a relationship to the whole that is coherent, but a fragment does not. As David Bohm pointed out: 'A part... is intrinsically related to a whole, but this is not so for a fragment... to fragment is to break up or smash. To hit a watch with a hammer would not produce parts, but fragments that are separated in ways that are not significantly related to the structure of the watch.'

The broken fragments of a watch are different from the parts that can be put together to make a watch. They do not have a clear relationship to the whole structure of the watch. The 'assets' that comprised the investment packages were like fragments, not parts that went to make a sound investment. They did not have a clear relationship to the possibility of increasing the monetary value invested in them. They were inherently flawed. The investment bankers responsible for them did not have a balanced or 'measured' approach to what they were doing. Their practices led to the fragmentation of the wider economy.

Moreover the bankers acted without any apparent thought for the implications of what they were doing, or for the well-being of their client companies not to mention the millions of others around the world whose lives were impacted as the economy was destabilized. A Greek myth gives us a term for this syndrome which is Narcissism, named for the beautiful youth Narcissus, who was rather cold-hearted. The term Narcissist was used by Freud to denote one of the three main personality types he believed played out in people. Narcissism in the psychological sense is defined as an inferiority complex covered over by a superiority complex. In other words, the partial sense of self is covered over by the inflation of itself.

Many fell in love with Narcissus, but he disdained them all. One day, when bending down to drink from a pond, Narcissus catches sight of his own reflection, falls in love with it and spends all his time gazing at the reflection. He does not realize that the face he is gazing at is himself. And of course, he can never reach the beautiful youth in the pond, and eventually dies of unfulfilled longing and is turned into the flower Narcissus.

A Narcissist lacks empathy for others, and puts his own interests ahead of the wider community. When *Fortune* magazine started to investigate Enron's crumbling financial infrastructure, CFO Andy Fastow's private comment to the reporter was: 'I don't care what you say about the company, just don't make me look bad.' By that time it was a bit late, because Enron was on the brink of unravelling, whether anyone knew about its structural problems or not. His comments reveal the way the unbalanced, partial self can lose touch with reality. He is more concerned with the appearance, the reflection in the pond. Self-image is more important than the reality of a well-run and successful company.

But what the Narcissist is really after is the *cause* of the reflection, his deeper self. In a mistaken attempt to find this, he bolsters his self-image and cannot seem to get enough power, admiration, status, money. He never stops gazing at the pond: at the outer. But the bonuses, the titles, the praises from his codependents and the people who have to 'manage' him cannot make up for the fundamental problem, which is the inner void. And as a result, he becomes insatiable. The combination of the inflated identity, the intellect's runaway feedback loop, and the insatiable need for 'more' may bring initial success, but very often leads to a mess. When company executives are fuelled by an incoherent sense of self, and therefore suffer from an impaired ability to think, mis-action is piled upon mis-action, until the whole company implodes, like Enron.

The problems of inflation can turn a Narcissist into a full-scale tyrant if he takes over a country and has vast resources at his command, including an army and a secret police force. Many totalitarian leaders of the early to mid-20th century fitted this description – Hitler, Stalin, Ceausescu, Mao, Pol Pot. These men were able to entertain monstrous ideas, carry out monstrous acts. They were able to see other human beings merely as integers, units to be destroyed or exploited systematically and efficiently.

However, not only were these men destructive and inhuman beyond all bounds, they were also irrational, that is they acted without the quality of reason. Stalin had his most seasoned army officers murdered just as the storm clouds of World War II were gathering. Hitler gave orders for Germany to be raised to the ground in his final days. Ceausescu had vast canal systems built which went nowhere. The nightmare regimes they presided over therefore lacked measure and proportion and *meaning* from every vantage point (including the hideous and titanically scaled architecture and public art they sponsored).

In his analysis of the flawed sense of identity that can arise in human beings, David Bohm once remarked: 'We generally behave as if the ego regarded itself as the universal "I am" beyond all limits of time, space and conditions.' These leaders were indeed men who behaved as if they were beyond all limits of time, space and conditions in every way possible and the destruction they caused was on a similar scale.

Chapter 13

The Fall in Consciousness

Our Constitution was made only for a moral and religious people. It is wholly inadequate to the government of any other.
John Adams

These are the fallen, who have forgotten everything
but how to fill the void with themselves.
This is the race that wants to rule the world.
And they stamp on parade, they creep like ice
indifferent to the tide, glacial as chemicals,
these are the ghouls that feast on us, feeling nothing
this is the planet of No Heart our children will inherit,
until we break the trance.
Jay Ramsay from 'Diabolic'

The loss of the connection to the inner self, and the compensatory inflation leading to mis-action, is what I believe is symbolized in the story of the 'Fall' found in the early chapters of Genesis. Adam and Eve were placed in a garden planted 'eastward in Eden' to 'dress it and to keep it'. They were the stewards of the garden, but something goes awry in their experience: they eat fruit from a forbidden tree, and the garden of paradise is lost to them. This action and its result is known as the 'Fall'.

The fall is in consciousness. We feel a diminishment, a 'fall' from grace. If we translate Adam and Eve as mind and heart (or intellectual and intuitive mind), this ancient text starts to reveal itself as a parable about identity that parallels almost exactly the Buddhist teachings:

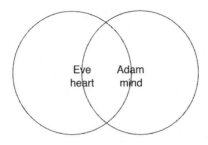

When Adam and Eve, mind and heart, are functioning in balance, all goes well. But their relationship turns 'dysfunctional' if the intellectual aspect of mind takes over, and the feeling perception from the inner becomes diminished. The beginning of this 'dysfunctional behaviour' in consciousness is depicted in the infamous conversation between Eve and the serpent, when the serpent successfully 'tempts' Eve into eating the fruit from the tree of the knowledge of good and evil. Adam and Eve have been told by the Lord God that they can eat fruit from all the trees in the garden except this one:

> for in the day that thou eatest thereof thou shalt surely die.
> Genesis 2:17

This does not mean: in the instant you eat this fruit you will drop dead. 'In the day' means a cycle of outworking, a visit to the museum, a decade, a lifetime. And 'die' means not doing so well, not feeling generative or confident. Ailing – the experience of the diminishment of life as opposed to the increase of life.

However, the serpent manages to persuade Eve that this is not really what will happen: 'And the serpent said unto the woman, Ye shall not surely die', in fact you will become 'as gods':

> For God doth know that in the day ye eat thereof, then your eyes shall be opened, and ye shall be as gods, knowing good and evil.

The literal-minded interpretation of this passage is that god didn't want us to get as smart as him, but to keep us in a state of naive subservience. But reading this as a dramatized story about how consciousness can malfunction, the phrase 'as god' carries echoes of the inflated identity that arises when we mistake our partial self for the whole self or, in Bohm's words, when we see ourselves as 'the universal "I am" beyond all limits of time, space and conditions.' The serpent is telling Eve that this is how she is supposed to operate.

The tree of the knowledge of good and evil grows in the centre of the garden. But so does the tree of life:

> the tree of life also in the midst of the garden, and
> the tree of the knowledge of good and evil.
> Genesis 2.9

Both trees grow in the 'midst of the garden'. In fact, they are the same tree, or two different aspects of the same process. One tree is the inner pattern, the other is the manifest, and both are essential aspects of the same dynamic. This is indicated a little further on in the Genesis text when Eve describes only one tree: 'the tree which is in the midst of the garden'. The repetition of the phrase 'in the midst of the garden' emphasizes the central importance of this understanding.

When we function in balance, we can utilize both aspects of this tree. We weave together the information and analysis of our intellect, with the fresh perspectives and feeling perception of our intuition. There is an easy movement backwards and forwards between inner and outer awareness. As a result, we produce 'seed-bearing fruit', ideas that work. We live and create in a generative, growing garden. But if we override the pattern of the inner, and eat the fruit of intellectual analysis of the phenomenal world only, we 'die'. We don't function so well, we don't think so well.

Eating this fruit also indicates the way our thought process and our identity become taken over and defined by the outer world. We 'eat' its fruits, we become part of it. We equate identity with the personality self, and think of ourselves as the sum of all the influences from our birth and background. We say we 'are' Irish, or Italian, we 'are' black or white, male, female, Muslim, Jewish, or we 'are' an intuitive type, extrovert, introvert, or the product of very ambitious but working-class parents, or of emotionally repressed parents, etc. We also identify ourselves with our jobs or roles – I am a lawyer, a teacher, a mother, and so on. We forget about the larger potential of our inner self.

The serpent in the Genesis text is the equivalent of 'defiled mind': the inflated self has set in and is now exerting its influence over our emotional perception. Instead of the intuitive awareness of the larger order of identity, and the balanced view that brings, we are going to substitute the intellectual ability to 'know good and evil', to discriminate, to judge, to divide up the world.

However, we will be doing this on the basis of an awareness that is itself already partial. Therefore we will discriminate and divide on the basis of that partial vision, not a whole vision. We will mistake money for wealth, confuse statistics with people.

What the Buddhists rather gently term the 'error' that results from 'defiled mind' is expressed much more forcefully by the Genesis story in which the results of the 'Fall' are catastrophic and life gets a lot tougher for everyone: 'Thorns also and thistles shall it bring forth to thee,' and, 'In the sweat of thy face shalt thou eat bread.' The impact is systemic and wide. This is inevitably going to be the case because the problem is created out of the very functioning of consciousness, and therefore its effects will be woven into the fabric of everything.

To those millions who slowly made their way through the financial fallout of 2008, it was literally true that the impact of the bankers' partial identities and self-serving actions were systemic in this way. Homes were foreclosed, student loans went up, there were less jobs for graduates, therefore they were likely to remain in debt for longer. Others lost jobs, and with the disappearance of their income, they had less money to spend, which led to further loss of businesses and jobs. The whole world's economy was blighted, which also served to undermine democracy itself.

When identity diminishes, and the balance of intuitive mind is upset, we can no longer function and think accurately within the whole complex world we live in. So we become like the proverbial bull in a china shop, breaking up or missing altogether the subtleties and possibilities of truly generative undertakings. There is nothing wrong with dividing up the world in thought, in thinking strategically, as long as we can:

> view those things in a bigger context, namely from the point of view of that fundamental oneness or wholeness, which is at the bottom of all consciousness and its objects.
> Lama Anagarika Govinda

When we are whole, we view other people and the world around us that way. We begin to have:

> the experience or the knowledge that we are not only parts of a whole, but that each individual has the whole as its basis, being a conscious expression of the whole.
> Lama Anagarika Govinda

'A conscious expression of the whole': what a lot of meaning is contained in this brief phrase. The way we perceive, think, generate ideas, and treat others is born out of a whole identity not a partial identity. This 'conscious expression of the whole' is what is meant by the word 'integrity'. The Oxford Dictionary gives its primary meaning as 'the condition of having no part or element wanting; unbroken state; material wholeness, completeness, entirety.' This quality then came to be associated with 'soundness of moral principle'and 'the character of uncorrupted virtue'.

Therefore we can begin to see that morality emerges out of a whole identity; that intuitive mind is the inherently moral mind. When we lose that balance, we lose the moral centre of ourselves.

Morality cannot be mandated, and is not arrived at by following rules or ethical guidelines. This is a secondary, derivative meaning of morality because lists of dos and don'ts and legal definitions of ethical procedures relate to the intellectual functioning of the mind without awareness of the whole. There cannot be a series of moral formulae created to fit all cases. Instead, moral action emerges organically in response to the particular set of circumstances we find ourselves in as the measure of self aligns within us.

Chapter 14

Dust

If we are to go forward, we must go back and rediscover those precious values – that all reality hinges on moral foundations and that all reality has spiritual control.
Martin Luther King, Jr.

and without our being there
we're living in a driven dream
where Money is God

worship and security
until the bubble bursts
the rug is pulled –
it all falls through

till we start to see
we must have sufficiency
not greed, our wants and needs
hopelessly confused, fused

growth at any price –
resources privatized –
and money, our social currency
that only exists because we trust it
Jay Ramsay from 'Metanoia'

When we remain aware of the inner self, intuitive mind is 'dual' in the sense of open to both the inner and the outer. But when we lose this balance, what was 'dual' can now start to become 'duplicitous'. Saying one thing, but meaning another. Lying. Intellectual sophistry takes over as the moral centre falters:

'Let's bet on this hedge fund.'
'Hang on a minute, I'm not sure this is legal...'
'Don't worry about it – nothing bad is going to happen from being really smart.'
Ye shall not surely die.
'But – our primary business is not making any money...'
'That doesn't matter – we can pay back our debt out of leveraging our future profits that are on paper...'

Here goes the intellect, getting carried away by its own schemes, by its own cleverness and overriding what is known intuitively in the heart. The schemes proliferate, grow larger and begin to turn into lies. What is complicated becomes deceptive: Enron's deception of its employees and investors, the Structured Investment Vehicles, Credit Default Swaps and Securitized Assets dreamed up by the Wall Street investment banks become simple fraud. 'Your eyes shall be opened': you will awake from the deluded sense of any moral reason. 'And ye shall be as gods': that line of Goldman Sachs' executives, seated in front of Carl Levin during the 2010 Senate hearings, all of them in the prime of life, stone-faced, arrogant, without a flicker of self-doubt, assured of their unending smartness and their prerogative to evade the Senator's questions. You will be 'as gods, knowing good and evil', you will become masters of the universe, able to control things by dividing the whole into fragments: selling mortgages to people who can't afford them because the immediate profit makes you rich, breaking down viable companies and selling them off piecemeal for short-term profit.

In simple terms, this is the syndrome of 'feeling the quantity' and not the quality of what we are creating. We override wisdom for the lesser meaning, we substitute the part for the whole, because quantity is only one half of the equation that makes up value. Quality is the other. Yet to state it in these terms distorts the reality of what is involved. Because quality cannot be quantified by a mathematical formula; and it does not arise from intellectual efforts alone, but from out of the depths of the implicate order. Selling quantity in its stead is trying to make up for the loss of wholeness by multiplying digits. We thought it was a bargain, to get more like this, but it was a scam.

The serpent in the Genesis story is a seducer, someone who tries to sell you something for more than it is worth. The serpent, the defiled mind that is now duplicitous instead of dual, is offering back to us only half of what is important, of what gives meaning to life. True, those executives and investment bankers made some people millions of dollars initially, and took home fat bonuses themselves. But ultimately they wrecked their companies, undermined their own clients; ensured that millions of people no longer had money to invest or buy goods with; and crashed the economy. It's a shoddy deal, a depleted version of what we already had: a thriving company, a buoyant stock market. We get more, but we are only getting *half*. Money made out of selling toxic securities is not the same as sounder investments that build up an economy instead of destabilizing it. More of half is not the same as less of the whole. Duality become duplicity shrinks the world down into something less than it really is.

Senator Carl Levin accused the executives of Goldman Sachs of acting out of 'unbridled greed' when they engineered the financial packages that contributed to the Wall Street meltdown. 'Unbridled greed' speaks once again of the inflated identity's need to aggrandize itself, which it does by carving up the world into meaningless fragments. The partial identity is not able to think in ways that take into account values which remain essentially general and unquantifiable in terms of intellectual analysis. Things like human dignity, trust, the importance of relationship, of community, the beauty of the natural world and the importance of a balanced ecosystem. None of these things show up on the bottom line, and none of them register particularly with the rapacious intellect under the thrall of the inflated self.

What this means is that values as well as morals are linked to identity. The loss of wholeness in ourselves leads to the loss of wholeness in the world around us, to unethical behaviour, to depleted values. We increase short-term gain at the expense of the long-term well-being of others; we extract 'commodities' from the environment to buy and sell, no matter the impact. There is a saying: 'Fools rush in where angels fear to tread': blinkered by our over-simplistic mechanistic view, we blunder into the fine-tuned interrelationships of the natural world, ripping out forests and hedgerows, filling up wetlands, and introducing crude chemical compounds and species of plants and animals whose very genetic code we have tampered with.

We 'fall' from the interior intuitive order of meaning. We lose grasp of intangible values.

Philosopher Ken Wilber calls this malaise 'Flatland'. He points out that all the great spiritual and religious traditions and teachers past and present share a common message that we as individuals have an interior dimension of self. In other words, there is more to us than the exhibit in the London Science Museum would have us believe. But in the 'Flatland' malaise, this inner, deeper dimension of self has been discounted and forgotten.

KW: ... in the modern West, we can't help but notice that all of the higher, transpersonal, spiritual levels of consciousness are looked upon with grave suspicion and even outright hostility. In fact, the worldview of scientific materialism, which is the 'official' worldview of the modern West, aggressively denies not only the higher stages of consciousness... but the existence of consciousness itself. The only thing that is real is frisky dirt.
Q: Flatland.

The absence of a sense of interior dimension of self has led ultimately to a society and a popular framework without any way to conceive of what value is:

> KW: ... [this] agenda awoke one morning to find to its utter horror that it was living in a thoroughly disqualified universe – a universe utterly bereft of value, meaning, consciousness, quality, and worth.

Written in the late 20th century, to me these words of Wilber's carry echoes of the extremely ancient Genesis text when the serpent is cursed:

> dust shalt thou eat all the days of thy life.

Dust: 'Frisky dirt'! Author John Anthony West, in his book *Serpent in the Sky*, explains that in ancient Egypt the symbol of the winged or flying serpent represents the consciousness that had a dual capacity: 'The serpent, seemingly a unity, is dual in expression.' In other words the dual nature of intuitive mind that can operate in both 'worlds' or dimensions:

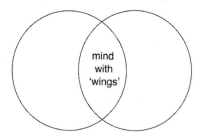

When consciousness can move freely between both worlds it is the 'winged serpent'. But when it becomes 'defiled mind' it loses its wings!:

> upon thy belly shalt thou go,
> and dust shalt thou eat all the days of thy life

Awareness 'falls' into only one level or dimension – the 'dust', the earth, the manifest, and suffers a corresponding shift in identity. This is how paradise is lost!

When our awareness and identity 'falls' we find ourselves expelled from the garden. The wording in the St James' text is very specific. The garden is described as 'planted *eastward* in Eden'. 'Eastward' means that which comes first, the place where the sun rises, the energetic pattern that precedes physical form – the implicate. While Eden is the realm of the manifest, the explicate. The 'garden' that is 'eastward in Eden' means the world revealed to us when we see as a whole consciousness. 'And a river went out of Eden to water the garden.' The river of life, the flow of love, of joy from our inner self that brings the world alive. This garden hasn't actually gone anywhere, *but it needs our consciousness to reveal it.*

No matter how much 'frisky dirt' we may get our hands on, without the flow of life-bringing joy and fresh perspective from the inner, we will never know real fulfilment, we will remain insatiable, like poor Narcissus gazing forever at what he cannot reach.

Chapter 15

Money-Scapes

When I'm working on a problem, I never think about beauty. I think only how to solve the problem. But when I have finished, if the solution is not beautiful, I know it is wrong.
R. Buckminster Fuller

We're lucky, we have shops, bars, a town square,
somewhere to walk to it's not like that everywhere:
windows tinted the vans slide past, no need to wave,
shuttles to Starbucks, soccer from the set-back shades
of houses that would like to be mansions –
evergreens, ornamental maples, mono-lawns –
swingset optional, hoop and the double garage
required, where the kids' social must-haves are in charge
to survive, and it could be woodland but isn't
and it could be a neighbourhood, but it isn't –
too close and too far apart – and the dogs all bark
they have a lot to say, but with you there's no spark
just call hi, how are you and move past smilingly
complete I don't know how a people grew to be
so frozen lonely, not even nosy, they don't
really want to know the price you paid, what you won't
do for a living anymore, they don't want to
know you at all...
from 'Walk In Somewhere and Return'

The uncoupling of heaven and earth brings the human world crashing down into the one dimensional 'Flatland' in which many of the values that give meaning to life do not appear to exist, or are not understood.

Over the last few chapters I have looked at how identity diminishes without access to the inner self, causing loss of perspective and proportion, and issues of Narcissism, with its lack of regard for the well-being of others. Entangled with these problems is a confusion about what value is, so that money alone, and the material lifestyle it buys, become the sole determinant of meaning. We literally evaluate ourselves by having the biggest house, car, bank balance. Or by building the tallest skyscraper (I sometimes think skyscrapers are metaphors for the attempt to reach back up out of 'Flatland' into the 'heaven' of inner values). Material success has its place, but when it is the only determinant of meaning, it gives rise to actions that lack 'measure' in both a practical and moral sense. David Bohm defined the way the ancient Greeks conceived of measure, contrasting it with the modern, more mechanical notion of measuring or comparing one thing against another: 'When something went beyond its proper measure, this meant not merely that it was not conforming to some external standard of what was right but, much more, that it was inwardly out of harmony so that it was bound to lose its integrity and break up into fragments.'

The meltdown of Enron; the Wall Street madness. Interestingly the tallest building (to date) in Western Europe is called The Shard, which is another word for fragment. This very expensive fragment (it cost 450 million pounds to build), which towers over London's skyline, had difficulty finding tenants for its offices and its luxury apartments remain unoccupied.

Values are abstract, but they show up in form all around us. And architecture is a form in which we can literally see them. If we walk down the western nave of Chartres Cathedral, for instance, and gaze up at the vaulted ceilings, we see an embodiment of harmony. We are impacted by an interplay of architectural feature, proportion and perspective and the way light interacts with all these qualities of space as it shafts in through the multifaceted stained-glass windows. Every part is in meaningful relationship to every other part, as well as to the whole structure and even to the cosmos. For instance, the height of the tower bearing the sun symbol is 365 feet, which is the same as the cathedral's length, and the number of days in the calendar year; the other tower has a moon sign, and is 28 feet shorter: the average number of days of the lunar cycle. We walk through an embodiment of coherence. And even if we are not aware of the intricacies of its design, the space can evoke a sense of coherence in us as well.

Chartres, like other great medieval cathedrals of Northern Europe, as well as mosques and ancient temples in other parts of the world, incorporates the shapes of sacred geometry into its layout and spatial design. Its ground plan, for instance, is based on the vesica piscis symbol in such a way that the centre point of the building corresponds with the centre of two giant intersecting circles:

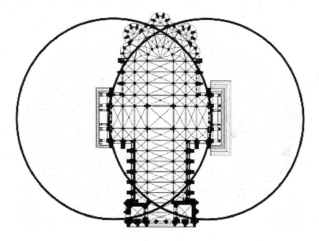

In his book called *Harmony*, HRH Charles, Prince of Wales, goes into more detail about Chartres:

The windows also conform to this ['vesica piscis'] shape. The great Belle Verrière window, for example, which depicts the Madonna and Child, sits perfectly within a vesica and thus perfectly within the floor plan of the cathedral, with every significant point in the design of the window corresponding to key positions in the geometry of the rest of the building.

All the design elements of Chartres are generated out of its fundamental ground plan vesica. As I explored briefly in Chapter 3, the quality of harmonious and proportional relationship between parts is encoded in the forms of sacred geometry, and this is why the builders and designers of ancient, classical and medieval times used them in the construction and design of their great architecture. They understood that harmony and balance emerged out of the marriage of heaven and earth, of an invisible and visible order, as evidenced in the forms of nature. And the 'temples' that they constructed celebrated this relationship and the web of coherence it produced, making the vesica the root shape not only of sacred geometry but sacred architecture as well. Symbolic meaning and geometric design were linked, deliberately. They were expressions one of the other.

Clearly The Shard was not built to celebrate balance and harmony. However, while it may be flamboyant, overpriced and underutilized, it has at least been designed. It can pass for architecture. But the same cannot be said of the majority of modern urban and commercial development, particularly in North America. Even the word development is a euphemism, because most of the time what one is really talking about is sprawl: the cookie cutter sameness of large chains and mega-malls and grid-like inner city apartment blocks and projects. These sites have not been developed in the sense of aesthetically designed and thoughtfully integrated but developed in terms of turning acreage into a money-making venture for as little cost as possible.

What is fascinating about these places is that as we try to interact with them, whether simply by looking at them, finding our way around them, or living in them, we get to experience the *absence* of those unquantifiable values which have been left out of the equation, and in their place, to come up against the incoherence and constriction of 'Flatland'. How often have we had to battle our way over windswept open parking lots, towards an anonymous-looking monolith, and cannot find the entrance because the building has not been designed to make that obvious? Or driven round and round in city traffic to find the entrance to the multi-storey carpark, that also has not been clearly integrated into the design? We all know how muggings and drug dealing were given almost perfect conditions by inner city housing developments, with narrow concrete walkways, and no human-scaled common space for the inhabitants to experience their community.

Proportion and perspective are qualities that require the sense of meaningful relationship between parts. As I have been exploring, it is possible to think and act in ways that lack proportion and perspective. But proportion and perspective are also visual elements needed to make designs aesthetic, or to give us a sense of relatedness to them. We know that we respond visually to the proportions and patterns encoded in sacred geometry and the golden mean because the same proportions and patterns govern the design of our bodies. This is why most of us prefer to walk down the nave of Chartres Cathedral, or through woodland, than across the wastes of parking lots and strip malls. One research experiment consisted of people being shown ten different rectangles. Most preferred the one whose sides most closely approximated a golden rectangle. Golden rectangles inform the facade of buildings as varied as the Parthenon of Athens, Notre Dame Cathedral in Paris and the UN building in New York. Architects ancient and modern knew that these proportions embody a subliminal message about harmony, connecting us in to the reason why they were built in the first place. Buildings that are 'developed' without these qualities are difficult for us to relate to. The Co-op City tower blocks, for instance, which rear up in cliff-like walls behind the interstate crash barriers of the north Bronx, are hard to even describe because they are so lacking in any design aesthetic. Clustered in random groupings, 35 or more in all, they are several city-blocks wide and encircled by chain-link fencing. Their bulk is in relationship to nothing else; they are ugly in every sense the word can give to us, burnt-out shades of beige, brick and grey, small windows stencilled across them; no one can walk to or from them, you can only drive through the feeder roads on to the highway intersections.

Just as desolate in their own way are the miles upon miles of leafy and often affluent suburban neighbourhoods, where the houses are just far enough away from one another to feel disconnected, but still too close to be in 'real' woodland; where if you walk around, you meet no one, where instead people pass by in bulky sports utility vehicles with tinted windows, so you can't see them (they can spy on you though). However, there is nowhere to walk to – no corner shop, no pub or cafe. The towns have no centres for people to meet and be in relationship. Relationship is meaning, meaning is relationship, is community, is *aliveness*. Instead of a bustling town square, fronted by locally-owned small shops and cafes, there are strip malls anchored by the giant chain stores or vast covered mega-malls, interspersed with the cloned shack-like buildings of the fast-food franchises, their forests of turning neon signs lined up interminably on either side of two- or four-lane feeder roads. And of course you can't walk here either. Each separate mall or fast-food shack has its own entrance, so to get anywhere you have to drive, turning in to endless traffic, or waiting at innumerable lights.

You cannot walk anywhere, yet there is no public transport. So people don't meet on buses or trains either. Everyone is in their own separate little car bubble, which is why if you do see anyone in those uneasy neighbourhoods, they will say, like automatons, 'Hi, how are you,' and rush past with their eyes averted.

The confusion about value and meaning gives rise to an oddly literal-minded approach, which is usually founded on the depleted values of utility on the one hand, and money, or cost-saving, on the other. Yet even though utility is emphasized – let's build a box and a parking lot and highways to get there – this idea does not function well. The literal-minded, utilitarian approach seems unable to integrate function with design.

The Greeks were the first to praise 'the good, the true and the beautiful'. Beauty we have already explored, as expressing the quality of internal relatedness. Good means beneficial, uplifting; true means functional, strong, of right purpose. What's interesting about these qualities is that they apply to both physical things, like buildings, and abstract things like ideas.

It is easy to see why Chartres Cathedral could be described as beautiful, due to its qualities of proportion and relationship; but it is also good, because its space is uplifting, benign, spacious both literally and metaphorically; and it is true, because its design works, it is functional, and it serves a purpose that, for most people at any rate, would be considered worthwhile, i.e. as a place of worship and contemplation.

But mall-land and those endless anonymous suburbs are lacking all three qualities. They are ugly, they are bad in the sense of isolating or undermining us, and they are unsound or untrue because they are inefficient, and don't work very well; they serve only to fragment and dilute the authenticity of human experience.

It looks like it's a neighbourhood, but it isn't. It looks like a white painted fence, but it's plastic. It looks real, but it's fake. This habit of substituting the fake for the real, or a symbol for the act itself – hanging out a flag with a Hallmark pastel of pansies in the spring instead of gardening – is another symptom of the literal-minded approach, and a depleted sense of meaning. We want the immediate 'fruits' without engaging in the creative process that would yield them. Fast-food, plastic fences, neighbourhoods where you don't actually have to be neighbours. And this is where consumerism becomes a substitute for the intangible values that we are lacking. Bigger cars, houses, flat screen TVs accumulating around us as products of impaired meaning. 350 channels with nothing on them. And even when a good movie is shown, it's interrupted every ten minutes with five minutes of ads.

These depleted values and the places that serve them do not

nourish us as individuals, or as communities. Isolation – which is the extreme form of the absence of relationship – is one of the results. Isolation, and a sense of meaning*lessness*. This is where depression begins. This is where alienation begins, when a young man buys a gun – or a semi-automatic machine gun, as the laws allow him to – and shoots his classmates. He is giving expression to the desolation of meaninglessness.

Chapter 16

Violence, Spin, Madness, Guns

It is difficult for the common good to prevail against the intense concentration of those who have a special interest, especially if the decisions are made behind locked doors.
Jimmy Carter

The Dark King
Fear-laden, long ago the sky looked dark
enough to fall, memories of monsters,
caves, running horses ruled our blood, the stark
crimson constant molten flow of danger.

The connection was vivid but confused,
half-forgotten – we wanted to kill him,
lift his blight from off the land. From within
now reigns he mostly, a shadow suffused

across the networks, where did this wasteland
begin? A synapse snaps, then the broadcast
far and wide – we cannot rein in the past,
but must move out further ahead, expand

into that dark and find it the setting
for our blue orb, space of all well-being.

In the grail myth there is a Wasteland Kingdom which is presided over by a Wounded King. He has been wounded in the thigh by a spear, but this is a euphemism. In fact this king has been wounded in his testicles, he is impotent. His sexual impotence is reflected in the problems of the kingdom, where the crops fail and the cattle cannot reproduce. Ancient societies believed that the king and the land were one; that the king 'married' the land, so if the king ailed in any way, the land would lose its fruitfulness.

The mythic wound is another symbol for the partial identity, which feels diminished and lacking power. Attempts to make up for the diminishment mean that this wound gets reflected in schemes that do not work, and in moral and literal bankruptcy: the equivalent of the barrenness of the wasteland.

However, there is one further characteristic of the wasteland kingdom in the grail myth, also caused by the King's wound, which is perpetual war and conflict. The land is described as 'ravaged by war and conflict'. Certainly violence characterized the 'reigns' of the tyrant leaders of the 20th century – military aggression, mass executions, death camps, labour camps, starvation, censorship.

In the grail story, the only time the Wounded King feels any relief from his wound is when he goes fishing. The fish is a complex symbol, having associations both with the vesica piscis and sexuality. Suffice it to say for now, that the act of fishing in the myth symbolizes the cover-up actions of the inflation: the need to get more power, control, stuff, status at all costs to try to fill the inner void. Getting more this way provides a temporary relief from the sense of powerlessness, but it cannot restore balance and fruitfulness. No matter how far Stalin extended his iron-fisted reach, the former Soviet Union remained a wasteland: mired in inefficiency, bureaucracy and fear, its people oppressed by poverty and hunger. In their millions they were spied on by the NKVD, detained, tortured and killed, either by execution or from decades-long imprisonment in the Gulag. When the Berlin Wall came down in 1989 the world learned how the vast Soviet empire, so rich in natural resources and human ingenuity, had been demoralized, bankrupted and terribly polluted. The Wounded King cannot bring life to his land, only blight and destruction.

Western democratic governments, entangled with corporate

stakeholders, also seek to control the population, only instead of force, they use subtler means, employing international PR companies like Edelman and political lobbyists like Karl Rove to manipulate public opinion through buying the media. In the US the rigging of judicial, even possibly presidential elections, the subsuming of the role of politicians by special interests and the substitution of spin for coherent policy all contribute to the sense of meaninglessness. Meanwhile, the NSA fails to prevent terrorists but spies on us through our phones. The banks withhold loans after receiving billions of dollars through Quantitative Easing. Wall Street firms cheat us by insider trading and selling toxic investments. Interest rates on student loans are increased, while Sallie Mae's former CEO Albert Lord builds his own private golf course. For-profit prisons incarcerate poor young offenders for minor offences. Big profitable box stores pay such low wages their employees have to be subsidized with food stamps to survive. Food producers put profit before nutrition and healthy eating. Cigarette manufacturers sue Third World countries who want to put health warnings on their packaging. US Republicans cut or prevent universal healthcare but condone 'corporate socialism' whereby the oil, agricultural, computer, banking and industrial military industries are underwritten by government funding. The institutions and leaders we thought were there to aid and protect us turn out to be amoral to the point of madness. Like mess officer Milo Minderbender, from the novel *Catch 22*, who is so obsessed with making money that he bombs his own squadron for profit, many corporate and political leaders no longer nurture civilized values and democracy but are blithely undermining them both to make money for their short-term self-interest.

In July 2012, the elite of Qatari society and other dignitaries including the then British Chancellor George Osborne (presiding over austerity policies for the general public) gathered to celebrate the completion of The Shard on its prime London site. Writing about the occasion, *Evening Standard* journalist Richard J.

Godwin penned the headline: 'The Shard – monument to the real rulers of London': meaning the superrich and their political enablers. Godwin compares the 309-metre-high narrow pyramid of The Shard to George Orwell's description of the Ministry of Truth from *1984* which was 'an enormous pyramidal structure... soaring up, terrace after terrace, 300 metres into the air.' It too was visible from almost everywhere in the city. Unlike Orwell's fictional Ministry of Truth, The Shard is not embodying the mad excesses of a socialist totalitarian regime. Instead, in real life, it embodies the mad excesses of unfettered capitalism in which London itself – one of the world's great centres of tolerance and civilization – can be bought and sold and dominated by the money of a disinterested elite, who have lost the understanding of what meaningful relationship entails.

On a smaller scale, gun violence is another way we see the wounded king archetype playing out in modern times. Guns give a false but lethal power to angry men who are suffering from the wound of powerlessness. A gun is rather like a substitute phallus. It is unfailingly rigid, but instead of life-giving seed, spits bullets and kills people. Killing people is an extreme form of controlling them, of making them conform to one's own distorted self-image, yet another attempt to make up for the diminished sense of self.

When we hear about a gun massacre, we feel shock, horror and grief for the victims and their families, and renewed disbelief at the National Rifle Association's ability to stifle common-sense attempts to limit gun sales (spurred on by the corporate interests of gun manufacturers). We also know we are witnessing the absolute nadir of human experience. We find it hard to conceive of the depths of despair and isolation that would drive someone to commit such an atrocity. Part of the horror we register is due to the apparent randomness, the lack of meaning. The culture of consumerism and manipulation, with its strip malls and isolated neighbourhoods on the one hand, and exploitative sleight-of-hand fake authenticity on the other, will not on its own bring someone to such an extreme, but it will feed back a lack of meaning into a psyche that, malnourished by the same depleted values, already feels fragile, alone, distrustful.

A more life-affirming culture and environment can help redress such psychic imbalances, but what can really make the difference in the shorter term is a meaningful relationship with another human being, whether a friend, therapist, teacher or minister.

Being in meaningful relationship with another person means we start to experience qualities like trust, friendship, kindness, even love. This is what heals us, not because the other person might be expressing those qualities but because *we* are. Meaningful relationship with another therefore puts us back in touch with the qualities of our own inner self. The 'therapy' of relating leads us back into relationship with our inner being, so that we are made whole again.

In other words, the way out of the wasteland is to heal the wound.

Chapter 17

The Ring of Dark Belief

Looking back, I see what a great influence an individual may have, even an apparently obscure person, living a small, quiet life. It is individuals who change societies, give birth to ideas, who, standing out against tides of opinion, change them.
Doris Lessing

We have been here before,
where the scorning reality
of our ultimate ineffectiveness
was blood-soaked into
all the backdrop of seeing,
and when the billboard consensus
of rational delusion
had utterly confounded us
into believing
we were on the surface
when we had already gone
under, pulled in the undertow,
barely breathing.
from 'At the Surface'

The wasteland of barrenness, incoherence and violence is reflecting a wound. The partial sense of self fuses into a half-articulated feeling conviction: an inferiority complex, a poor self-image. The sense of unease becomes a buried but corrosive belief that one is unworthy. Nothing is worse than this dark resignation ruling within us.

When a belief is profoundly negative, it can create the condition that ultimately causes someone to gun down innocent bystanders.

This is because a negative self-image turns us into an addict. An addict is someone who abuses something in order to try to ease an addiction. In the case of the gunman, the addiction has to do with power. He feels powerless, and to make up for it, tries to control others through violence and the power of the gun.

The only time the Wounded King feels any relief from the pain of his wound is when he goes fishing. The problem is, the more he fishes, the more wounded he becomes. The more an alcoholic reaches for a drink to make him feel good, the more he needs it. The more we need other people to validate us, the more violent we will become in our attempts to control them. The more we need status and money to give us meaning, the greater the risks we will take to achieve our ambitions. This is called a vicious circle. Round and round it turns, unless we can break out of it. I call this syndrome the anatomy of the wound:

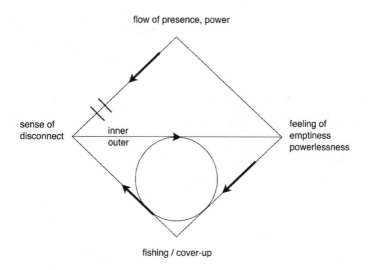

The Anatomy of the Wound

When we disconnect from our inner self, the sense of well-being seems to falter. We feel partial, empty, powerless. To compensate, we go 'fishing', we seek substances, tangible and intangible, from the outer world to try to fill the void. But the more we consume, the deeper the entrenchment in the partial awareness, the deeper the negative feelings become and the greater the need to relieve them. One person becomes a Narcissist, another becomes a codependent. Often they meet up. Some have to control others, or feed their 'wound' with an excess of money. Some become dependent on people, others on material substances, such as alcohol or drugs. Whatever the manifestation, the same circuitry runs underneath addictive behaviour of all kinds.

I think this spinning circle of misery is what was symbolized by Tolkien when he described the fearful 'ring of power':

One ring to rule them all, One Ring to find them,
One Ring to bring them all and in the darkness bind them.

The same pattern is at work, underneath all the different ways it plays out. It *is* a powerful ring. In Tolkien's story, even when the wizard Gandalf throws the ring into Frodo's fireplace, it is not damaged, but the heat of the fire does reveal its markings. The fell language of Mordor is seen running around its golden rim. The markings of this dark language are like the negative beliefs that can hold us in their thrall, beliefs that the circle of addiction – the ring of power – sustains in our experience.

Not all beliefs are negative of course, or buried so deep. Some of our more positive and consciously owned beliefs morph into values: a list of qualities or intentions that we try to live by. Similar values and beliefs may be evoked in religious and civil ceremonies such as marriages or christenings. Or they may be encoded in law. For the most part these belief-based values and laws are reasonable, and help us live together and build a complex and civil society. But there is always the danger that they turn out to be unjust. Laws that made homosexuality a crime, for instance, or which limited voting rights for African Americans in the southern states of America.

Unjust laws like these, and the struggle that is often needed to change them, are related to the way our values can turn back into beliefs which are tangled up with the sense of who we are. It was astonishing, for instance, to witness the amount of prejudice and hatred targeted toward President Obama because his racial heritage is part Kenyan and his middle name, Hussein, is common in Muslim cultures. Again, the problem arises when identity is overly defined by the personality self, and not the deeper self. Then a person's values/beliefs become part of who they think themselves to be, and therefore to question those values, is to question them, or make them wrong. This is when we can become polarized around over-simplistic ways of framing the world into right and wrong, which in turn often become bound up with ethnic, racial, gender or religious conflicts. When polarization sets in, reason leaves. Worse still, when values/beliefs become part of one's identity, they can also become a 'cause' which that person will fight for, and attempt to impose on to others. From the medieval Crusades of Europe, to Apartheid, to modern day attacks on abortion clinics in the US, to the censoring of common-sense debate due to political correctness. The attempt to impose our values and beliefs on others, to have them think the way we do, is another form of the attempt to control people instead of being in relationship with them. Another form of violence.

An unquestioned or buried belief is like a default setting. We are no longer aware that it exists, and so we interpret its 'settings' as our reality. Therefore we tend not to question how we see things. Here's David Bohm again:

Reality is what we take to be true. What we take to be true is what we believe. What we believe is based upon our perceptions. What we perceive depends upon what we look for. What we look for depends on what we think. What we think depends on what we perceive. What we perceive determines what we believe. What we believe determines what we take to be true. What we take to be true is our reality.

To break the circle, we have to let in new meaning. This means we have to access once again the relationship to our inner self, so that new insight moves in to our awareness. Unjust laws change as our beliefs change, and our beliefs change as the sense of who we are changes.

If the nadir of human experience is depression, hatred and the sense of powerlessness that erupts in meaningless violence, the zenith is what we call love. As I already explored, love itself is not so much an emotion as it is the core frequency of ourselves, but it is through our emotions that we experience the extent to which we are aligned with love or pinched off from it. We pinch ourselves off from the force of love when we harbour beliefs that are discordant to its frequency, that are not true of us. The more discordant the belief, the more negative the emotion. The more benign the belief, the lighter the emotion. This means that the painful emotions we feel are really symptoms, warning signs of the disconnect from love. Ultimately, as we move closer in awareness to our source, we can more or less dispense with beliefs altogether. This is how the ring of power is dissolved in Tolkien's story. It is thrown into the fiery molten river in Mount Doom. The fiery river symbolizes the flow of love which has the power to dissolve both the negative beliefs and their circle of addictive or limiting behaviour. Then, instead of rigidly adhering to or defending our beliefs we participate in the continual emergence of new thought, new ideas, new ways of seeing things. Instead of homosexual men and women being shamed for their sexual orientation, we have Gay Pride walks. We see through the eyes of love.

Chapter 18

False Certainty

Violence is the last refuge of the incompetent.
Isaac Asimov

History is full of people
who were sure they were right

like the bold dreams
of the settling Puritans
and their covenanted church.

They founder on the smallprint
of orthodoxy, their minds
locked in precision argument,
rigid with old hatreds
for those who deviate.
from 'It Could Have Been Different'

The ancient motif of the Wounded King and his Wasteland Kingdom is found within the grail myth and threaded through the stories of King Arthur. And by presenting us with two kinds of leaders and two kinds of outcomes, these legends help make explicit the link between identity and leadership. The Wounded King symbolizes the leader who functions as a partial self; King Arthur the leader who functions as a whole self; the former rules over a wasteland kingdom, the latter over a united and prosperous kingdom.

In one sense we are all leaders, because we all lead our own lives. Moreover, we live within widening circles of relationships with others: our partner, our family, our local community, the organizations we work for and so on. Depending on how we function as individuals, we affect these wider circles in constructive or destructive ways. We are the apex of our world. Even if we are at the bottom of the company ladder, we are still the head of our version of that company. But if we find ourselves the actual leader of an organization: a neighbourhood group, a business, a nation, then our impact is potentially greater still.

If we list the attributes of the whole self that I have explored so far, we find that they are also the attributes of good leadership: balance and perspective; blending intuitive insight with intellectual analysis of complex factors; creativity; the ability to see differently, to bring new meaning to a situation, to free up from myopic beliefs; a moral centre; values that include but go beyond the bottom line or short-term fixes; open-mindedness, compassion and measure in relating to others. Equally, the traits associated with the partial self are also those of corrupt, tyrannical or ineffective leadership. I have already looked at some extreme examples of the Wounded King at work. The Narcissistic leadership of Enron, and investment banks such as Goldman Sachs, whose culture of reckless self-interest and expansionism wrecked people's livelihoods and crashed an economy; some of the dictators of history, such as Stalin, Hitler and so on, whose destructive schemes went beyond all bounds of what is recognizably human, and were irrational to boot; the attempt to control people, whether through violence or manipulation and schemes to rip off citizens instead of helping them grow and develop. But the Wounded King syndrome can also manifest itself in more chronic ways, yet still cause immense 'wasteland' problems due to the individual's position of influence and power.

One of the problems, as I have been exploring, when we function as a partial identity is that our ability to think is impaired. Without the fluid, subtle intelligence founded on the ever-shifting relationship of meaning between inner and outer awareness, we have difficulty grasping complex situations. We tend to default to certain fixed ideas, often closely connected into personal beliefs, which in turn are blended into our sense of identity. In this way our thinking is shaped more by the past, by precedent than by what might be emerging now. Additionally, the inherent inflation of the partial identity means that conviction replaces open-mindedness, essentially closing us off from other points of view, particularly if they oppose our own. Under pressure we entrench. We become Right, with a capital R, and therefore everyone else, unless they agree with us, becomes Wrong.

Conviction is no substitute for coherent insight and informed overview. This might be one of the lessons to be derived from the 2003 invasion of Iraq by George W. Bush, a Wounded King leader who never doubted his decision. Even though no definitive evidence linked the September 11 attacks with Saddam Hussein's leadership, and even though there was no substantial intelligence about the presence of Weapons of Mass Destruction in Iraq. The attacks on the Twin Towers were shocking and unprecedented, but the cause of them was not clear at the time, and seems even less clear as time goes on. Certainly, the 'good' versus the 'axis of evil' framing of the situation by the Bush regime was inadequate to appreciate the complexities of Arab states such as Iraq and Iran. Similarly, the strategy for the war suffered from a lack of serious and detailed consideration of what would follow the major, opening offensive. It is almost household knowledge that countries where tribal and religious sects have long histories of rivalry and injustice, held in check only by a strong, often brutal dictatorship, are going to splinter when that control pattern is removed. How could such a situation resolve itself overnight into a peaceful democracy? It was an astonishingly over-simplistic idea. But of course, the vision of creating democracy in the Middle East was heavily tainted with securing control of the oil reserves. This was the longer-term aim. Yet this opportunism seemed only to lend greater urgency to the mission, thus contributing to, rather than offsetting, the lack of foresight. And so the situation deteriorated into predictable chaos as the initial euphoria of some Iraqis passed, the experienced leadership, tainted by association with Hussein, were in hiding or hunted down, and underlying rivalries and factions took over the streets, fighting both each other and the American soldiers and their allies.

Bush's certainty only added to the problem, as he proved himself incapable of, even unwilling to, comprehend and take in the true complexities of the situation. He remained polarized and mired in his right versus wrong model, confusing his 'side' with the right, and unwilling to listen to advice from others including – in a triumph of ineptitude – that of Secretary of State Colin Powell, one of his most experienced advisors, whom Bush effectively froze out and undermined.

Bush often appeared to be the inexperienced and somewhat lazy puppet acting as the good-looking, affable front man for the cabal of hard-line right-wingers who, looking to the past, wanted America to flex its authoritarian muscles again on the world scene. But he had his own version of their vision, wanting also to be great in the eyes of his father perhaps, and, added to this, had undergone a religious experience, from which he emerged feeling he had a personal connection with Jesus. Unfortunately, his emotional experience and ideas meshed together into the belief that Jesus had wanted him to be president. This belief cemented his obduracy, as it meant his conviction was backed up by the son of god. In medieval Europe, this attitude was enshrined in the sovereign as the divine right of kings. The idea was that the king or queen had been appointed by god, and therefore his or her decisions and actions were above question because they were sanctioned by divine authority.

However, there is a crucial difference between the belief that we are hearing divinely ordained ideas, and the actual experience of connection to our inner self. The former is another variation on inflation: 'Ye shall be as gods'; the latter is the wisdom of alignment. But when we have an idea that we hold to strongly, and which is forged by powerful emotion into an unquestioned belief, the result is a kind of false certainty. And this can seem compelling. To begin with anyway, there may not appear to be much difference between this false certainty, and the intuitive 'lining up' of the fundamental relationship of meaning. Even in ourselves, it is sometimes difficult to tell the difference. We can fool ourselves or fool others. However, it need not take very long to notice that there is a difference. The false certainty has an oddly garish glow to it, we or others seem too positive, too confident in an unbalanced way. And we will easily turn defensive or evasive. The true line of measure means that we are open to question, open to let our insights be developed, checked out. We want to build something that really works, not just pursue an agenda. And finally, one can look around at what actually happens: 'By their fruits ye shall know them.' Do we create a wasteland or a living system? A creative outcome or a mess?

An intriguing piece of symbolism that bears on these ideas is the story from Exodus of Aaron's rod. Moses has appointed the Tribe of Levi to be the priesthood, but another tribe argue the job should be theirs. To resolve the dispute, Aaron and the leader of the other tribe both leave their rods in the tabernacle overnight. In the morning they find Aaron's rod has flowered, signifying that his tribe is the rightful priesthood. Both rods look the same from the outside, but only one can produce flowers. Conviction and alignment might look the same, particularly during the razzmatazz of an election or dressed up in Karl Rovian spin, but only one can produce results. This symbolism picks up the theme of sexual potency again, the rod that flowers is the phallus that can deliver the life-giving seed. The Wounded King or partial identity leader cannot do this, he has lost connection to his true power, he is impotent, ineffective. And therefore, to make up for this, like the vengeful gunman, he resorts to violence. He goes to war.

Chapter 19

Kennedy & the King Arthur Myth

Any intelligent fool can make things bigger, more complex, and more violent. It takes a touch of genius – and a lot of courage – to move in the opposite direction.
EF Schumacher

I love those times
when everything
I think I know
dissolves

When the paving stones
and buildings
of solid assumption
turn suddenly old
and collapse

And I am left newly outside
in the blue shock of the biting air.
from 'New Bearings'

The Wounded King rules over a Wasteland Kingdom, where the crops fail, the cattle cannot reproduce and where the land is ravaged by war and conflict. King Arthur presides over a united kingdom, in which his Knights seek noble deeds that bring renown to the realm. President Kennedy, who himself has almost become a legend, has long been associated in popular references with King Arthur. The musical *Camelot* had opened on Broadway only weeks after Kennedy's election, and as well as becoming a big hit, had also been apparently a personal favourite of the Kennedys'. Its music and spirit seem to have pervaded to some degree the atmosphere of their White House. And after Kennedy's death, Jackie Kennedy had actually insisted that the writer Theodore White evoke a connection between Kennedy's brief era and the promise of an idealized Camelot in his essay about the late president for *Life* magazine.

Depending on one's point of view, the association with Camelot is either a deft piece of propaganda or a poignant truth. Certainly one essay cannot explain the impact of Kennedy's assassination on so many people, not just in the USA, but worldwide, and the way the lost promise of his presidency haunted several generations of Americans. Camelot was the fabled castle that housed the round table where the Knights of the Round Table would gather. The round table is a symbol of brotherhood and noble purpose, of coming together to do good on behalf of the wider community. Kennedy exuded charisma and a sense of optimism, and he inspired a spirit of service and possibility. The spirit of those who asked not what the country could do for them, but what they could do for their country: the Peace Corps volunteers, the NASA scientists and technicians who implemented Project Mercury aiming to put a man on the moon, and the Civil Rights advocates who fought to end segregation in the South.

But there was another, and I believe more significant, reason why the association between Kennedy and the Arthurian myth persists, which is that he was a truly effective leader. He was the aligned leader who not only presided, albeit briefly, over a flowering of possibility and progress, but who steered the country, and in fact the whole world, away from the brink of nuclear war.

The Cuban Missile Crisis of 1962 was triggered when US spy planes photographed nuclear capacity missiles in Cuba. Kennedy knew he had to act, he had to do something. But he was perplexed at what appeared to be a hugely escalatory action by Khrushchev, when the latter had given him assurances this would never happen. As well as a dire threat, the action was a puzzle. What was Khrushchev's motivation? How could he find out? Action that was too extreme would simply trap both leaders into further escalation and war with a terrifying potential outcome. What was the deeper meaning?

In his memoir *Thirteen Days* Robert Kennedy is at pains to stress that his brother, the president, sought out advice and input from as wide a range of people as possible. Those in positions of high command, those on the ground, those who presented differing or unpopular points of view, who would raise questions and criticize regardless of rank or viewpoint. Kennedy tried to think through not only the first steps, but the manifold consequences of any opening steps. He had to think globally, because action taken in Cuba might result in reprisals in Berlin. He had to think about the possibility of a nuclear war and the cost to not only the existing population but future generations. And he had to look at those same issues through the eyes of his opponent.

The movie of the same name *Thirteen Days*, based on Robert Kennedy's memoir, reconstructs the pressures that came to bear on the President during the crisis. In one scene he meets with the Pentagon hawks, bristling not only with military expertise and nuclear strategies but (some anyway) with the unshakeable conviction that they needed to strike first. Kennedy simply listens, thanks them and leaves: when they had expected an immediate, action-based response. In this way, the film dramatizes how Kennedy was able to counterpoise the weighty arguments to embark upon nuclear war with his own presence. True, his role as President and therefore Commander-in-Chief gave him authority over the generals, but he also drew on the authority of his own poise. He neither ignored the advice from the various experts, nor became hostage to it. In fact the White House tapes, released in 1997, record that at one point Kennedy alone, amidst all the voices of his team, not just the army chiefs, was standing out against hard retaliatory action.

Instead his leadership was able to create a space in which, with the help of his advisors, Khrushchev's letter, the halting and withdrawal of Soviet ships from the blockade and through Ambassador

Dobrynin, he began to read the deeper meaning of what was happening. He realized in fact that Khrushchev himself did not wish to go to war, but was partially hostage to his own military. In other words, Khrushchev's situation in some respects paralleled Kennedy's. This understanding allowed Kennedy to navigate through the tangle of mutual brinkmanship and de-escalate the situation – without either regime losing face.

Kennedy's leadership during the Cuban Missile Crisis demonstrated two almost contradictory components of effective leadership: the willingness on the one hand to listen to a wide range of input, and the ability, on the other hand, to avoid getting caught up in limiting structures of belief that might distort the complexities of the current reality. Here is the balanced approach of intuitive mind at work, in which input and strategic options are weighed against a personal intuition which dictates timing and waits to see what the deeper issues are.

The ability to disentangle from the structures of pressure, expectation, precedent, and to draw back from all the assumptions thrown up by the circumstances is beautifully symbolized in myth when Arthur draws the sword Excalibur from the stone. Written in gold letters around the sword is a prophecy that whoever can free it is king of all England. The sword represents our power, our leadership potential, and in order to lead we have to be able to free ourselves from, or cease investing our power in, the structures and pressures that surround us.

In some versions of the King Arthur story the sword is stuck point down in an anvil on top of a stone. Iron and stone are both hard, rigid materials and these two layers – one smaller and closer in, one larger and further out – represent our personal belief structures and those of the larger systems in which we function. In other words, the symbolism of drawing the sword out of the stone is another metaphor for alignment. Instead of being embedded in the outer, we are freed up to let the flow of insight from the inner bring new meaning to those outer structures and circumstances.

The belief structures symbolized by the anvil and the stone are not necessarily all 'wrong'. The advice, insights and experience of Kennedy's advisors were not wrong or irrelevant. But becoming overly involved in them carries the risk of not seeing the larger picture, and the deeper possibility. As soon as Arthur draws the sword out, he becomes king. The anvil and stone transform into the kingdom. A kingdom is the world which gives us allegiance because we make it coherent. The structures, input, conditions and advice that surround us can be given new meaning and relevance when we balance their content with the insights from the inner.

Many stronger, mightier and more experienced knights than Arthur (in fact at this point, Arthur is not even a knight) had tried in vain to wrench the sword out. Yet Arthur was the true king – he was king by birth, but his ability to draw the sword out demonstrated that he was the king by his openness to the inner realm as well. Many of those advising Kennedy were far more experienced in their fields than he was. But he demonstrated that he was the best able to lead because he could bring new insight and perspective that in the end steered the whole scenario to safety.

The symbolism of the sword parallels that of Aaron's rod. To free the sword is a variation on the theme of a-lign-ment, representing the ability to let the unit of fundamental measure form within us, so that as leaders we carry potency. We are the real thing, not just the appearance.

Chapter 20

A Round Table

Afterwards the Round Table was set up on Merlin's advice, and its establishment was not without significance, for it was called the Round Table to signify the roundness of the world. And the situation of the planets and the elements in the firmament, and in the circumstances of the firmament can be seen the stars and many other things; so that one could say that the world is rightly signified by the Round Table.
from *La Queste del Saint Graal*

A thin coronet of gold
is all there is to hold
the kingdom

To draw a circle
and then widen it:

a circlet of gold
on fine hair

a castle of old
upon the tor

a belly swelling
to birth.

'Please, move your chairs,
widen the circle',
the man called.

from 'The Coronet'

Kennedy's willingness to listen to input from a wide range of advisors is another characteristic that links his leadership with the Arthurian theme. The contribution of each one was valid, regardless of role or rank. Whether it was the fighter pilot's eye-witness report of events on the ground in Cuba, the advice of his Secretary of State, or the input from the American Ambassador to the UN, no one could tell ahead of time which bit of information or insight was more or less important in synthesizing an overview and figuring out what to do.

The pooling of this collective intelligence is one of the possibilities represented by the Round Table, where the knights are invited to sit as peers with King Arthur, each with equal access to its centre. They all have different skill sets, expertise and roles. Each one brings a different perspective and this spectrum of viewpoints and experience can contribute to filling out understanding of whatever the issues are. The effective leader values and seeks to draw out this collective input, just as Kennedy did, because he has the service of the larger whole at heart, and not a narrow or over-personalized agenda.

Where Kennedy sought to engage people's skills and experience, and elicit their insights, Bush attempted to control and censor, hearing only what suited his preconceptions. While Bush divided the world into good and bad, and evoked the rhetoric of an 'axis of evil', Kennedy acted on behalf of the whole, the whole planet ultimately, and instead of casting his opponent into the role of arch evil-doer, was able to see into his mind. He reached out to negotiate in every way possible, he acted with restraint and intuitive intelligence and proved his quality by standing up for the greater good, making that more important than national ego. Then he made it safe for Khrushchev to do the same. His leadership steered the outworking away from the brink of nuclear war, and toward a condition of greater stability.

The mythical King Arthur epitomizes the quality of great leadership for the same reasons. It was not because he carried out stunning heroic solo acts, but because he set up the Round Table and united the Kingdom. This is the modality of the whole self, not the partial self. The aligned consciousness that can perceive and evolve new meaning, blending information from the outer world with insight from the inner self. When we stay in balance this way, we find the path through the maze, the steps to take that bring resolution. At the same time, our rootedness in the deeper aspect of ourselves makes us value the perspective of others. We can take in multiple points of view because we are not defensive about our own. Above all, as I believe Kennedy's leadership demonstrated, we are sensitive to the movement and possibility of wholeness itself, and therefore are able to generate the fruits of wholeness, such as peace and stability, in the circumstances around us.

Many groups and philanthropic organizations have taken the symbol of the round table to evoke their mission, including the Round Table organizations in Britain, whose equivalent in America are called Rotary clubs. These are people who have come together to do good on behalf of their communities, just like the Knights did good deeds for the Kingdom. Another contemporary echo of the myth are 'round table' discussions where teams or different stakeholders meet, often literally in a circle, for an inclusive discussion so as to get all viewpoints heard and avoid polarized agendas. At the United Nations, the delegates sit in a circle; as do the politicians in the European Union headquarters in Brussels, in an attempt to do the same.

While both elements, commitment to a noble purpose and the experience of coming together as peers, are symbolized by the Arthurian Round Table, they do not by themselves comprise the full potential of what the archetype means. The Round Table is a symbol of collective coherence. It evokes the field of generative possibility in a group, a company, perhaps even a nation, that can form under enlightened leadership, in which people feel both committed and empowered, knowing they are present as peers whose input is valued (but not indulged). This field often gives off an aura of excitement and power, a 'buzz' of renown that is due to its very nature. One former employee of Microsoft in the 1990s said that she felt 'anything was possible'. Again, it is the real thing, not just a PR campaign. Companies who have this kind of energy going are usually successful.

The field of collective coherence begins with a leader who is functioning as a whole self. He or she acts as the 'seed crystal' who can turn the chemical soup of a grouping into coherence. This process often begins with a strong partnership between the leader or founder, and one or two other key individuals. Their relationship acts like a creative field, which will become the nucleus of a larger configuration of people.

A field in its original sense means an open, prepared piece of land in whose ploughed and fertilized soil things can grow. If we connect two vesicae piscis shapes together their combined pattern symbolizes the way in which the relationship between two individual consciousnesses generates a whole that is more than the sum of its parts:

As separate vesicae piscis, there are just two fish or almond-shaped segments, one each! But when they interconnect, there are five, while smaller ovals are also generated out of the overlapping curves. We can think of this as symbolizing the evolution of a particular 'implicate order' of the relationship: 'as each person enfolds something of the spirit of others in his consciousness...' (David Bohm). The field of the creative partnership intensifies the process of 'growing' new meaning. All kinds of possibilities and ideas start popping up between us.

If one keeps on adding vesicae together, one ends up with a shape known as the Flower of Life. This shape can look like a complex flower head, or a collection of rounded flower heads of six petals:

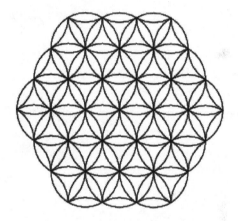

But if one looks more closely, it is possible to discern the series of intersecting circles that compose it:

Just as the vesica piscis by itself symbolizes a coherent individual consciousness, the Flower of Life symbolizes a coherent collective consciousness or field, that has at its centre a leader who is functioning as a whole self, and who encourages others to do the same. The whole field is much greater than the sum of its parts. Rather than a bureaucratic grid where each person knows their role and does not cross over into any other 'slot', there is a creative overlapping or linking of people and of their consciousnesses, creating a cultural connectedness that is systemic. The 'petals' that appear when this shape is drawn are once again symbolic of the new insights and possibilities generated out of this quality of systemic connectedness.

If we picture the mythical Round Table, King Arthur and his knights are seated together around it. There is a pattern of leadership present, as well as a complex set of interrelationships one to another. When a group becomes a round table, it is able to combine the dynamics of hierarchy with the overlapping and systemically linked collective field. The 'flower of life' within the circle:

Similar shapes are found carved on to a gypsum and alabaster threshold step from one of the Assyrian King Ashurbanipal's palaces, dated to 645 BCE (now in the Louvre, Paris); and in the Osirion temple complex in Egypt where it has been carefully drawn on one of the pillars in red ochre. The date of the drawing is most likely much later than that of the temple, some suggestions put it around 500 BCE – the time of Pythagoras.

Here I am in the Louvre, sitting by the gypsum
and alabaster threshold step from one of the Assyrian
King Ashurbanipal's palaces, dated to 645 BCE.

The interlinked quality of the group means it functions as a kind of self-organizing whole, in which ideas can pop up from anywhere within the organization. It is not about one person leading and the rest following in a linear way, but about the group figuring out together ways to fulfil their mission within the overall intention set by the leader.

A good example of this happening comes from the experience in 1966 of the fledgling United Farm Workers who, under the leadership of Cesar Chavez, were seeking to negotiate with the DiGiorgio Corporation (the largest growers of table grapes in the nation) through collective bargaining elections. Many of the new workers were sympathetic with the UFW's aims, but still too scared about losing their jobs to participate. In their book about collective wisdom, authors Alan Briskin, Sheryl Erickson, John Ott and Tom Callanan describe how the UFW have been barred from entering the camps where the workers live, barred from engaging in conversation with them and from discussing the workers' democratic rights to vote for the UFW to represent them. The UFW are on the roadsides at five a.m. handing leaflets through the slats in the trucks that are transporting the workers to the fields. But that is all they are able to do. Chavez calls a meeting, lays out the situation, says that he cannot currently see a solution and asks for input. Many people share ideas, none are rejected, the debate goes on a long time; then, when the meeting is almost over and a stillness has descended on the group, an old woman in a Mexican shawl who was seated at the back of the room stands up, and starts speaking quietly in Spanish. If they are not able to go to the workers, what about the workers coming to them? Why not build a small altar or church on the public roadway across from the camp entrance. The workers can come and pray with them, and that way they will get to know and trust them. Her idea is simple but radical, and it worked. Chavez parked his station wagon outside the camp gates and put up a small altar in the back. At first only a few workers came, then many more, and when the election was held, the workers voted to have the Union represent them. The woman's idea was the seed that formed out of the collective field. Chavez himself did not come up with the solution, but his open-ended leadership allowed for a coherent field to form that helped catalyse her thought.

The gathering of collective intelligence – the input of many that Kennedy sought, the free flow of ideas and debate that Chavez asked for – means that we offer insight into the centre of the table. We pool our thoughts, our opinions, ideas, information, perspectives, etc, based upon our different viewpoints, roles, skills, backgrounds, experience, and so on. And then the centre of the table represents this pooling of information and the overview gained by it. But the deeper aspect of the round table experience is when the centre represents the collective presence that can synthesize new ideas out of the data. Briskin, Erickson, Ott and Callanan call this the experience of collective wisdom because they recognize that it gives rise to: 'a quality of group understanding that is neither of the intellect alone nor of any individual alone.' In other words, a collective version of intuitive mind forms in the group, allowing for a deeper level of insight than the merely strategic or linear. One process moves from the rim into the centre, the other process moves from the centre out to the rim. And probably there is a natural breathing in and breathing out that goes on constantly in groupings related to these two aspects of intelligence and wisdom, and the interrelationship between them, that together form the basis of the possibility of collective leadership.

Chapter 21

Dialogue & Collective Coherence

Every age has a defining characteristic. Ours is one of dialogue. Changes and innovations can only be successfully understood and implemented in the spirit of the modern age, to ensure understanding and coexistence among the peoples of this world on the basis of mutual respect. In this spirit, new perspectives of balanced development can be achieved for all peoples of the world without fear of injustice, hunger or disease, and where their children cannot be deprived of just sleep in the absence of safety and security. Therefore, I emphasize that the Qur'an advocates dialogue as the correct path for mankind.
King Hussein I

*And at the centre
of the citadel –
and we almost know now
how to let this happen –
like a lotus blossoming
in the square,
the aperture of ourselves
opening the way memory
breaks into flesh and color
when some well-loved person
or place is seen again.*
from 'No Temple'

In his memoir Robert Kennedy wrote about the problems inherent not only in a time of crisis, but in government in general, of working with such a huge amount of information. This is a problem for multinational companies and other large-scale organizations as well as governments. Today, the complexity of all the moving parts of undertakings such as military interventions, or drilling for oil in different parts of the world, or the manufacturing and distribution of goods, means the issue of handling and synthesizing information and evolving policy, even with the aid of computers, becomes ever more problematic, and can give rise to missteps and poor decisions.

Since Kennedy's time, the field of leadership studies has grown and proliferated, spawning an array of consultancy modalities which are aimed at helping organizations operate more coherently within this sea of information and complexity. One thread within this mix is systems dynamics and systems theory, particularly as evolved through the Sloan School of Management at MIT, which identifies some of the forces at play in large-scale organizations. In his ground-breaking book *The Fifth Discipline* MIT-based business luminary Peter Senge articulated five disciplines required to lead effectively in such settings. One of them he termed 'team learning', which he felt began with the practice of dialogue. Dialogue had been evolving out of the work of David Bohm, who, as much philosopher as he was theoretical physicist, was perplexed at the way human experience remained so fractured when, at the quantum level, all appears to be intricately connected.

Dialogue was birthed at a conference I attended in the early 1990s, when David Bohm and 40 others spent a weekend exploring his ideas in free flow conversation. During the weekend something of the experience of a coherent collective field began to form amongst us, and led to the idea of following up to explore how to more consciously facilitate this experience. Bohm believed there existed a flawed process of thought in human beings that both linked and gave rise to a confused sense of identity which led in turn to conflict and incoherent social conditions. Through the process of coming together in groups and dialoguing it was possible to move through the 'pollution' in thought, and end up in a different kind of space together. Building on Bohm's insights, those who pioneered much of the dialogue work in large-scale organizations identified this phase of the dialogic process as the point when the group shifts from being a collection of 'parts' or separate individuals and starts thinking and functioning as a collective whole, calling down a deeper shared flow of perception:

> This [stage] is the one where people cross over into an awareness of the primacy of the whole... It is also a place where genuinely new possibilities come into being... where people... are personally included but also are aware of the impersonal elements of their participation. In this fourth space, people have an experience of flow – often a collective flow. Synchronicities arise more often here: One person will think of something and another will say it. People become more aware, in essence, of the primacy of the undivided whole that links us all, and so notice it more readily.
>
> William Isaacs, *Dialogue and the art of thinking together*

This experience was seen as a potentially powerful tool to help leadership teams tackle the issues of overload and complexity. Instead of a collection of different perspectives vying for dominance, the team turned into a coherent collective intelligence, able to achieve an overview and allow new breakthrough ideas to emerge.

Dialogue involves people being together in physical form, in a room, and usually seated in a circle. It also works best when the leader or convener of the group is functioning as a whole self, and therefore acts as the seed crystal to help the group cohere. However, when we gather together like this, there is an additional catalyst, which is the group presence itself. There we sit, like the knights at the round table, with all our individual differences of heredity, roles and skills, and at the same time, there we also sit as a collection of inner selves. The inner presence of each individual already shares the commonality of being, and when we sit together, particularly when we sit in a circle, this commonality nudges at us. If we look around, it is the circle itself, rather than any individual, that dominates. Meanwhile the centre of the circle, which is usually more or less empty, acts like ritual space, evoking the potential of what we might be together. For those whose identity has been pretty firmly wrapped up in only one dimension of themselves, the intensity of this circle space can be uncomfortable, particularly to begin with. But the 'seed crystal' person is already conversant with this space, and speaks into and from it, acting like a catalyst or a magnifying lens that intensifies awareness of the group presence. Bit by bit a deeper dimension of being begins to permeate the group. This intensifies the pressure on those who are most disconnected from their own presence, and they can start to grandstand, trying to dominate the space. In Bohm's terms, this is some of that 'pollution' in thought showing up. The person is identified with their agenda, with their 'position', with their beliefs, and in the circle space where a new depth of presence is being felt by others, this limited thought pattern jars like a klaxon, announcing its own disconnect and inauthenticity. This behaviour will usually give way as the group presence, rather than any one person's personality, begins to dominate. Those tempted to use the group field as their sounding board either experience an internal shift, or are given no more oxygen because the collective field is now formed and tangible enough that it is almost impossible to ignore. If the process continues, a sense of oneness, connectedness descends into the group. The difference is palpable.

Now each person is a peer not just in terms of having their expertise and input equally valued but also in terms of each one having access to their own inner self as well as to the group presence. Each is free to expand and evolve new meaning out of the collective mix, unhindered by pre-existing biases or agendas. Otto Scharmer, Senior Lecturer at the Sloan School, MIT, and founder of the Presencing Institute, describes this experience and its potential:

Once a group crosses this threshold, nothing remains the same. Individual members and the group as a whole begin to operate with a heightened level of energy and sense of future possibility. Often they then begin to function as an intentional vehicle for an emerging future.

The ability to see the future, to sense new possibilities before they have taken full shape, is about the whole being greater than the sum of its parts. The field of collective coherence is forming an implicate order that is unique, specific to that grouping. Out of this new interior order, the seeds and insights for the future expansion are engendered.

Dialogue can be used to incubate coherence within an organization, but if the seed crystal of wholeness is not present in at least one individual the experience can be laborious at best, or the shift may simply never occur. Just seating everyone in a circle is not enough to achieve coherence. Without the lift of the inner dimension the mechanism won't work. However, it does not matter how coherent a smaller grouping or team becomes within a larger organization; they will not have much impact on the wider culture if the overall leadership is not also involved.

Chapter 22

Initiation by the Group Presence

I speak the word from which I was made.
Normandi Ellis, *Awakening Osiris: A New Translation of the Egyptian Book of the Dead*

Finding Your Voice
Finding your voice
is not a matter so much
of lunging about
trying on this lavish
gesture, this fully-
prepared phrase,
but more a question
of settling down
growing still
enough
to make the secret
steadying link-up,
when the words are offered
like elegant gauntlets
that fit, something
subtle and fine enough
something that does
your self justice.

The experience of sitting in a circle, which is integral to dialogue, and talking as peers caused a refocussing on circle gatherings that have always been a part of the way Native North American tribes sought to deliberate deeply together. And this in turn threaded a more explicitly spiritual awareness into the dialogue context because the native American tradition takes into account the will and movement of the Great Spirit. The Great Spirit informs humans, animals and the rest of nature, and it was understood that human beings needed to act in ways that were in harmony with this higher energy and larger whole. These ideas connect back to the Buddhist named 'universal consciousness', and the idea of conTEMPLating, weighing up one's ideas in the context of the harmonious cosmic web, only now the temple is the circle of people and the collective field. Similar practices and cosmologies exist of course in other indigenous sacred traditions, and there is also one famous account from Acts 2 in the New Testament of a group accessing a unified heightened energy together. This was the occasion not long after Jesus' crucifixion when the disciples had gathered in an upper room and found themselves together 'with one accord in one place'. The implication here is that not only were they in one physical 'outer' place, but also in one spiritual, inner place. They were with one accord, they had come into a depth of agreement that was not to do with agreeing about things but with a depth of connection together. As a result, they experienced a kind of fiery energy:

> And when the day of Pentecost was fully come, they were all with one accord in one place. And suddenly there came a sound from heaven as of a rushing mighty wind, and it filled all the house where they were sitting. And there appeared unto them cloven tongues like as of fire, and it sat upon each of them. And they were all filled with the Holy Ghost, and began to speak with other tongues, as the Spirit gave them utterance.
> Acts 2:1

Obviously this account cannot be verified and, depending on one's viewpoint, can be dismissed as religious propaganda or myth-making. But, if one makes allowances for different vocabularies and ways of speaking about hard-to-define experiences, this is not a dissimilar description to the account of one participant in a modern day gathering:

> There was a high-frequency energy being passed between people, and I could sort of see into people's minds. And there was a period of time where the whole group had a very discontinuous awakened experience, where we could basically perceive the same reality together but express it in each of our own unique ways.
>
> From Craig Hamilton's article 'Come Together! The Power of Collective Intelligence' in *What is Enlightenment* magazine, issue 25, May-July 2004

I can personally testify to experiencing such intensification of insight and energy many times in gatherings large and small. On one occasion, for instance, about 35 of us were gathered for a weekend conference to explore the practice and experience of Attunement, a non-touch healing therapy. We had been together for about two days, in plenary sessions and smaller groups, and were gathered for a more informal co-creative evening that included poetry and dance as well as comment. About two-thirds of the way through our time, I and others felt an opening and expansion of atmosphere. I described it as an energetic cathedral space revealing itself around us, and joining us in a dimension that was transcendent, beyond individual story, agenda or difference. For an interlude of possibly no more that 10 or 15 minutes, we were blended in a high frequency fiery connection together, that was full of love. Whatever the circumstances are that can call out these experiences, I have come to believe this dimension of group energy, to varying degrees of intensity, is an ever-present potential. Such experiences are not accessible only to an initiated few, but can be thought of as a natural part of our collective life as human beings.

Intense group experiences can act as a spiritual initiation for the individual. A participant in another grouping describes her experience:

It was almost as if we were suddenly surrounded by [an] ambient energy that allowed each person to leap, inside of themselves, into a much vaster way of being…

From Craig Hamilton's article 'Come Together! The Power of Collective Intelligence' in *What is Enlightenment* magazine, issue 25, May-July 2004

In other words, the experience of the collective presence amplified the individuals' awareness of their inner selves. It is as if they suddenly get to hear their own authentic voice, because the group field has helped amplify its tone. Out of the background cacophony of unhelpful influences and other 'voices in our head' we finally get to hear our deeper selves.

I have watched this process at work several times in groupings where a collective field is forming. I remember one experience at a women's weekend retreat, on our second day together; the facilitator had led us skilfully and delicately into a very deep field. It was as if it landed suddenly among us or opened suddenly beneath us. I found it remarkable in its clarity, and the clear before-and-after distinction in our collective experience once it had shown up. Another occasion was at an Art of Hosting workshop convened by organizational leadership practitioners to explore and teach ways to facilitate coherent group leadership. Participants attended ostensibly because they wanted to learn new leadership tools. But as the workshop progressed, a more fundamental ingredient of leadership was seeping in to them from the group presence, touching and opening this awareness more clearly in themselves, and it was this experience in the end that had the deepest impact.

There is an interlude in the stories of King Arthur that symbolizes the initiatory power of the group. The knights are at Camelot, gathered together with King Arthur at the Round Table, when the grail suddenly and mysteriously appears. Covered with a cloth of white samite, a semi-transparent material that veils its appearance, the grail moves around the table, and offers each knight a taste of what they most desire. Then it disappears, leaving each one longing for more, so that they all vow to embark on the quest to find it. What the grail offers the knights is this taste of their own authentic presence, which is supremely satisfying. We may get a taste of our inner self in a high-energy collective setting, but if we are going to know this experience more directly and consistently in ourselves, without the amplifying effect of the group, we have to go on the quest to find the grail and view it directly, without its covering veil.

Chapter 23

Inside the Grail Castle

Knowing yourself is the beginning of all wisdom.
Aristotle

Here Comes the Meaning of it All
It all happens at once – always the way –
inside that banqueting hall, candles, fire
the distinguished host, how it all conspires
to make you wonder what to do, to say:

and then the sword, magnificent, gifted
what to make of it, next the veil – lifted:
here comes the meaning of it all, the grail
whose radiant light makes the great room pale.

Whom does it serve? That's the riddle: watch now
it moves past from one room to another
we are watching our own selves, this is how
we feel when our heart fills with the power

of love, we line up, the sword is mended
and better still, the wasteland is ended.

The taste of what we most desire is the presence of our inner self becoming known. We are filled with this, it is an embodied experience, not an intellectual one. And so the golden chalice is a symbol of our heart when it is filled with this presence: 'my cup runneth over', the feeling of love spilling over and flowing out from us. This is a transforming power, it transforms us and the way we see the world. And so subtle and yet so profoundly significant is this process, what Rilke called a 'direction of the heart', that it has the world's most beautiful and enduring myth dedicated to it, which is the myth of the grail quest.

Like many other myths, the grail story has a number of variations to it, including the episode when it mysteriously appears at Camelot, and a great many versions exist in medieval literature. But the oldest and most resonant version of the story features a naive young knight Perceval, whose very name means to pierce the veil. And it is worth exploring the symbolism of this story because it dramatizes both the moment when we feel this presence and why it is crucial that we do.

Perceval has been brought up in deepest Wales, far from civilization and unaware of the glittering courtly world of knights. But one day while out in the woods surrounding his home, he comes upon five knights who dazzle him with their splendid appearance. He vows to set out at once for King Arthur's court, to become a knight himself. This is devastating news for his mother, who has kept him deliberately marooned to protect him because her two older sons were both killed as knights. But Perceval will not listen to her remonstrances, and heads off. He finds his way to the court and is knighted by Arthur. He also overcomes a fierce Red Knight, who has been terrorizing the court, and takes the Knight's red armour for himself. Perceval then meets a kindly and experienced knight named Sir Gornemant, who trains him in knightly skills and in etiquette, advising him not to talk too much so he does not betray how unsophisticated he is. Perceval sets off again, and this time comes across a beautiful damsel named Blanchefleur whose castle is under siege by two wicked knights. Perceval fights and overcomes her besiegers and sends them back to King Arthur to change their ways. However, even though he and Blanchefleur are now sweethearts, he will not stay longer because he feels compelled to return home and reassure his mother that he is well. He also can't wait to show off to her his shiny new red armour.

But Perceval's next encounter, and the central scene of the story, is something altogether different. For Perceval finds himself in the castle home of none other than the mysterious Wounded Fisher King. This is the King whose wound is reflected in his Wasteland Kingdom where the crops fail, cattle cannot reproduce and there is continual war. However, Perceval does not yet know this. And there is something else he doesn't know either, which is that the way to heal this King is to find the grail, and then ask the question: whom does the grail serve? This is all that is needed not only to heal the King, but also to restore the Wasteland, because of course as the troubled Kingdom is merely a reflection of the King's wound, once he is healed, it will cease to be a wasteland and become fertile and prosperous again.

Perceval is led into a splendid banqueting hall, hung with tapestries and lit with candles and a great fire, where he is invited to sit beside the Wounded King. During the sumptuous meal that follows, a door to an adjoining room opens, and a lovely maiden enters carrying the grail. As the grail enters, a great light fills the space and Perceval watches, mesmerized, as it is carried across the hall, and into a second room on the other side. The grail is so beautiful, and the light it brings so intense that Perceval desperately wants to ask about it and find out who is served from it. But, ringing in his ears is the advice his mentor gave him not to talk too much. And so, fearful of appearing impolite or doing the wrong thing, Perceval overrides his desire and does not speak.

The light which the grail brings symbolizes the epiphany when our heart feels the inner presence. What makes this happen? The grail moves from one room through the hall to another – its movement represents a shift in our attention from one realm to another. The two rooms flanking the hall represent inner and outer awareness. When we loosen our involvement with the outer world, we connect to the inner. In fact the layout of the grail castle echoes the shape of the 'vesica piscis', and the emergence of intuitive mind:

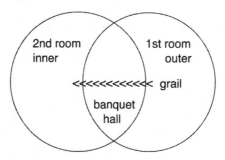

Within the sacred architecture of our own consciousness the chalice of wholeness is found. We feel the connection as the line of fundamental measure forms, and personality self and inner self come into new relationship.

If we, like the more resistant participants in dialogue or other circle groups, are unused to feeling the connection to our inner self, the experience can be disorienting. After all, up until now, we have been focussed outwardly, guided by people who inspired us or goals we aimed for. We have believed that for the most part meaning lay outside ourselves: in our skills and roles, in our achievements and in our relationships. And the same has been true in Perceval's experience; his goals and aims have all appeared to be external to him, bit by bit drawing him away from his childhood home, and out into the world.

Now, suddenly, we find meaning bursting upon our awareness from within, altering the world around us. And we will often try to talk ourselves out of paying it much attention because its implications are so unsettling. To paraphrase TS Eliot, we may have had the experience, but we're not sure we want to explore its meaning. We want to remain normal, after all. And this reluctance is dramatized in the story by Perceval remaining silent.

If Perceval had asked about the grail he would have learned that inside the second room, into which the grail is taken, there lives an elderly man with white hair whose nature is so refined he can live on the white wafers served to him from the grail. I call this figure the Grail King. It is he who is served from the grail:

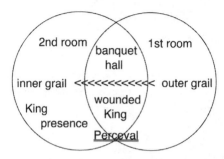

And of course, the Grail King represents the inner self, our presence. And the grail serves him. Our heart is the instrument of our inner self, the feeling perception by which we experience the nature of love. It is this presence that fills us once the door to the inner is 'opened'.

Even though like Perceval we may not be ready to take on the full implications of the epiphany, we have still been changed by the experience. The scene symbolizes the dawning in us of conscious awareness about our inner self. The moment when we realize that meaning lies inside as well as outside of ourselves. Govinda describes this as an 'inner conversion… the re-orientation, the new attitude, the turning away from the outside world of objects to the inner world of oneness, of completeness.' This experience is described in the Lankavatara Sutra as a 'turning-about in the deepest seat of consciousness'.

The symbolism of the grail castle is literally synonymous with the image from the *Mahayana-Sraddhotpada-Sastra* that describes intuitive mind as having: 'two doors from which issue its activities'. When the door to the inner, to the second room where the Grail King lives, is 'opened' the full circuitry of intuitive mind emerges. The presence of our inner self floods into our conscious awareness and, as this happens, the condition of 'defiled mind' is healed. The Wounded King is healed.

The outer world that was a wasteland is now made fertile again by the flow of renewing energy from within, and in turn the flow back from the living world brings the refinement of beauty and essence, the white wafers, to nourish and expand the implicate level.

Once we touch in to this experience, we cannot revert to unconsciousness and act as if everything is the same as it was before. Or at least, we cannot try to do this with impunity.

The episode in the Grail Castle marks a turning point for Perceval. Up to this point in the story he could in a sense do no wrong – he has sailed along on that current of ease which helps us attain things when we have no preconceptions that we cannot. Winning the red armour is like buying the red sports car with the proceeds of our early success. But as Perceval's experiences mount up, he is becoming less unworldly, more skilful, and at the same time, a little more conditioned. He loses the moment of epiphany: the banqueting hall is silent, the fireplace cold and the door to the inner room will not open to his knock. The vision has shut down, and from then on it seems as if he can do no right.

Perceval leaves the deserted castle, hoping to find its occupants out hunting, but instead comes upon a maiden grieving over her dead lover. She inquires where he stayed and whether he saw the grail, then tells him that if he had asked about the grail he could have healed the Wounded King, and by healing him, restore the Wasteland. Now the Wasteland would persist and it is all his fault! She also tells him that his mother has died of grief at his absence. Perceval is overwhelmed with sorrow, guilt and confusion. However, due to the many wayward knights Perceval has sent packing to King Arthur's court during his adventures, Arthur sends for him, and holds a banquet in his honour. But at the height of the festivities, a hideous hag appears and repeats even more vehemently the accusations of the grieving maiden. All Perceval's achievements and good deeds – becoming a knight, overcoming wicked knights, rescuing maidens – mean nothing in the face of his failure to ask about the grail.

The story has a comic symmetry to it. Perceval's mother from the first part of the story, who was adoring but overprotective, is replaced in the second half by the accusatory hag, who lays in to him without mercy; and instead of his gentle sweetheart Blanche-fleur praising him for rescuing her, now the reproachful grieving maiden tells Perceval all the things he's done wrong. The mother-turned-hag and the sweetheart-turned-complaining nag are both female, one old, one young. They appear in their baleful form in the second half of the story as the heart's emissaries. They are telling Perceval that if he doesn't listen to his heart, nothing else he does will have much value. If we do not make the feeling connection to our inner self we will not heal the condition of 'defiled mind' and restore the incoherence it produces. And therefore, instead of dealing with the root cause of the wasteland, we'll continue to place Band-Aids on its symptoms.

Even worse, if we fail to pay heed to the epiphany but remain convinced that meaning lies outside, we risk turning into the Wounded King ourselves. Perceval is invited to sit next to the Wounded King. He shares his couch. He is drawing close to the King, vulnerable to his influence. We may find ourselves headed down that shadow path, needing more and more status and bonuses and 'stuff' in order to shore ourselves up. And as our identity begins to inflate, the wasteland will expand.

There is a process in all our lives whereby we need to grow not just from innocence to experience, but from innocence to wisdom. Perceval is characterized as an innocent fool, impetuous and unsophisticated. In fact, this is why his mentor had advised him not to talk too much, lest he give himself away. After his encounter in the Grail Castle, Perceval's job is to become wise.

Most of us have probably experienced the way people can change from thinking we were marvellous, to seeing only our faults. This reversal happens when we fail to make the shift from innocence to self-awareness, fail in fact to act on what we know. What may have been cute or easily overlooked when we were setting out in our innocence, becomes irritating in the extreme when we are old enough to be self-aware. At the same time, if we do not learn how to let intuitive mind emerge, and to therefore balance input from others with the promptings of inner direction, we can begin to either doubt ourselves and give our authority away, or become obdurate and unreasoning, closed to any input. Either way, the more we do this, the more annoyed people tend to become, particularly those closest to us. They know us best, like mothers or lovers tend to, and so can appear to turn from those who most nurture us to those who can most undermine us.

After the hag excoriates him for remaining silent, Perceval realizes finally that he is on a quest, and must find out whom the grail serves. However, the process is not instantaneous. He experiences five years of futility, searching for but not finding the Grail Castle. This is when life begins to seem hard, when despite our achievements and skills, we no longer feel inspired. Perceval never finds the Grail Castle again, but instead meets a wise hermit, who tells him about the Grail King in the inner room. Therefore he comes to understand the answer to the question, which symbolizes our conscious understanding that we have an inner self. This is the understanding which will help us regain our joy and excitement about life, and become wise as well.

Wisdom in fact is this self-awareness; and the consequent ability to draw on both intuition and intellectual analysis, so that we think and act coherently.

Chapter 24

Joining the Worlds

Blessed are the pure in heart, for they shall see God.
Matthew 5.8

An empty room I didn't realize was there
in the centre of my being
where I am with You.
So many other rooms, a palace of faces
but without this
there's no well inside,
above and below.
So in my innermost heart and soul
I must say 'I am that I am'
I can surrender,
and I can command
I can say
'I love you, I am sorry, please forgive me'
to this heart
'for creating a reality separate from you'.
And so I bow,
and because I can bow
I can command.
from 'Confession' by Jay Ramsay

Perceval must fulfil his name, and 'pierce the veil'. When 'defiled mind' is in place, there is a veil between our personality self and our inner self:

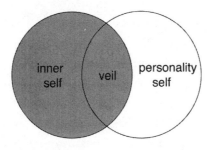

To pierce this veil is to connect to the inner self. Then the balance and clarity of intuitive mind emerges:

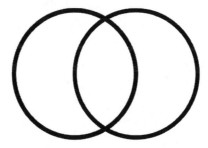

A veil is semi-transparent, it allows a diffuse awareness of what is behind it, but this is not yet clear. So the veil both joins and separates at the same time. When we pierce the veil, we end the separation between inner and personality self, which was really only perceptual anyway, not actual.

We experience the epiphany, we find we are the light source. We feel whole. The grail quest depicts a developmental process, whereby we become aware of the inner dimension of self. It is a journey of self-discovery. As I have mentioned, this process can be catalysed by a high energy group presence, or by a person, place or even a work of art. We can also stumble on the experience for no apparent reason. But the grail story tells us that just having the experience once or twice is not enough; we need to consciously understand what is happening and apply it in our lives. One way we do this is through some form of meditation. The aim of meditation is to become still, because by quieting thought and involvement with the outer world, it is easier, to begin with anyway, to become aware of our presence and the renewing flow from the inner. Practising meditation is also called becoming 'mindful' – our mind becomes full of the awareness of presence, as opposed to full of distracted thought that is reactive to our circumstances.

Becoming mindful, we realize that meaning*fulness* exists inside ourselves as well as outside. That in fact, we bring meaning, we light up the world around. The reason for this is that the world around us is contained in our consciousness. There is no other way in which we perceive anything manifested except through our consciousness. Back in 1928 the British physicist Sir Arthur Eddington wrote: 'It is necessary to keep reminding ourselves that all knowledge of our environment from which the world of physics is constructed, has entered in the form of messages transmitted along the nerves to the seat of consciousness...'

Everything that we see and think about the world is 'inside' our heads. We cannot cut our consciousness away from that world. The world has always been inside our consciousness, but when we become aware of our inner self, we start to realize this fact. Not only do we realize that the world is in our heads (as far as we are concerned, that is) we also experience or *interpret* that world differently. For one thing, when the light is strong, the dimensional world seems lit up, heightened. Like the moon, it glows with reflected light. The light, the sense of well-being is moving out through and from us, altering that world. And therefore, we come to notice that the world, the apparently very material world, is permeable, fluid; that it is affected deeply by the quality of our consciousness and of our attention.

Heisenberg is famous as a physicist for formulating what is called the uncertainty principle. Part of what this means is that if we determine the position of an electron, we cannot also know its velocity; and if we determine its velocity, we cannot know its position. We see it differently, depending on how we look. In this sense we literally impact the world, or the way it appears to us. But more broadly and deeply, we impact the meaning of the world by the way we attend to it. If 'defiled mind' is in place, if the king is wounded, the world will reflect that, because without the flow from the inner to illuminate and bring it alive the world will seem like a wasteland to us. And then, due to the malfunctioning of our consciousness, we will start extending the wasteland through our thought and action in all the ways I have explored in this book. The ancient myth is true: the king and the land *are* one. Our consciousness and the world are one. Meaning and matter, as Bohm understood, are intermingled.

It turns out that when we pierce the veil, we join not only our inner and outer selves, but the inner and outer worlds. We join heaven and earth. In this way, we undo the spell of illusion that had us believing they were ever separate.

Up until the experience of 'turning around', the epiphany in the Grail Castle, it has never occurred to us to question our assumption that the world was separate from us. Feeling separate ourselves from the inner, we interpreted everything else on that basis, viewing the world as a measurable, ultimately completely knowable knock-on-wood material reality that we use our intellect to analyse and extract what we want from. But we are intermingled with the world, and we must pattern it in our likeness. The living pattern of coherence is configured in our own mind, our own identity. When we live between the vastness of heaven and the beauty of earth, coherence in our thought, in our relationships, in our policies and social structures will follow.

Notes/References/Bibliography

Introduction: Whole People Produce Whole Outcomes
Nicolás Gómez Dávila quote from *Notas 1*

Chapter 1: Who Am I?
Aphorism by Novalis (1798) from *Pollen or Fragments*, translated by Charles E. Passage
'Two Worlds' from *Between Two Worlds* (Chrysalis Poetry, 2014)
Lama Anagarika Govinda, *Foundations of Tibetan Mysticism* (BI Publications PVT Ltd., 1994 Indian reprint)

Chapter 2: Template
Immanuel Kant quote from *Critique of Practical Reason*
'Temple' from *Between Two Worlds* (Chrysalis Poetry, 2014)
Einstein quotes from Intuition-Indepth:
http://intuition-indepth.blogspot.com/2007/11/einsteins-intuition.html
Ralph Waldo Emerson quote from his essay 'Self-Reliance'

Chapter 3: Opening a Pathway in Thought
For information about the vesica piscis as root shape of sacred geometry, the origins of philosophy, and the mathematical proportions of nature's patterns, and for drawings and more I drew on Michael S. Schneider's *A Beginner's Guide to Constructing the Universe: Mathematical Archetypes of Nature, Art, and Science* (HarperPerennial, 1995).

Chapter 4: Unbroken Wholeness
Lindsay Clarke quote from *Imagining Otherwise* (GreenSpirit Pamphlet No. 6, 2004)
'The Art of Wholeness' from *Between Two Worlds* (Chrysalis Poetry, 2014)
David Bohm, 'Soma-significance and the Activity of Meaning'

from Chapter 3 of *Unfolding Meaning: A Weekend of Dialogue*, edited by Donald Factor (Routledge and Kegan Paul, 1985, 1987)

Lama Anagarika Govinda, *Foundations of Tibetan Mysticism* (BI Publications PVT Ltd., 1994 Indian reprint)

David Bohm, *Wholeness and the Implicate Order* (Ark Paperbacks, 1983)

David Bohm, 'On the intuitive understanding of nonlocality as implied by quantum theory', *Foundations of Physics*, volume 5, 1975

Chapter 5: The Measure of Self

Lama Anagarika Govinda, *Foundations of Tibetan Mysticism* (BI Publications PVT Ltd., 1994 Indian reprint)

David Bohm, *Unfolding Meaning: A Weekend of Dialogue*, edited by Donald Factor (Routledge and Kegan Paul, 1985, 1987)

Michael S. Schneider, *A Beginner's Guide to Constructing the Universe: Mathematical Archetypes of Nature, Art, and Science* (HarperPerennial, 1995)

David Bohm, *Unfolding Meaning: A Weekend of Dialogue*, edited by Donald Factor (Foundation House Publications, 1985)

Chapter 6: The Owl Appears

'The Prayer & the Creation' excerpt from *To the End of the Night* (Northwoods Press, 2004)

William Blake quote from the poem *Auguries of Innocence*

Carl Jung, Volume 8, 215 of *Collected Works*

Samuel Taylor Coleridge, *Biographia Literaria*

Lindsay Clarke from a talk entitled: *Anima Mundi: The Soul of the Earth*, 7 July 2013, Subscription Rooms, Stroud, UK; part of a series of live literature events run by Kevan Manwaring and Jay Ramsay of the Awen Forum.

See also: Lindsay Clarke, *Imagining Otherwise*, GreenSpirit Pamphlet No. 6

Chapter 7: Seamless

'Art' was one of the poems featured in the shop windows of Keene, New Hampshire, as part of the Keene Literary Festival of 14–15 September 2012, organized by New Hampshire Poet Laureate, Alice Fogel, and sponsored by the New Hampshire Writers' Project; it was first published in *Amethyst Review*, edited by Sarah Law, April 2018.

Michael S. Schneider, *A Beginner's Guide to Constructing the Universe: Mathematical Archetypes of Nature, Art, and Science* (HarperPerennial, 1995)

Christopher Alexander, *The Luminous Ground*, Book 4 of *The Nature of Order*, Center for Environmental Structure

Gerard Manley Hopkins quote from 'On the Origin of Beauty: A Platonic Dialogue'

Chapter 8: Love & Meaningful Relationship

Vincent van Gogh quote from his letter to Theo van Gogh, The Hague, 21–28 March 1883

Excerpt from 'See Clear Through to the Sun' first published in *Diamond Cutters: Visionary Poets in America, Britain, and Oceania*, edited by Andrew Harvey and Jay Ramsay (Tayen Lane Publishing, 2016)

Chapter 9: The Path Through the Maze

'Thin Places' from *Between Two Worlds* (Chrysalis Poetry, 2014); also published in Witches & Pagans magazine, June 2015

For the images and information about Malekulan Nahals I drew on: Patrick Conty, *The Genesis and Geometry of the Labyrinth* (Inner Traditions, 2002)

Jill Purce, *The Mystic Spiral* (Thames & Hudson, 1974, pp. 120–121)

Drawings derived from A. Bernard Deacon's *Malekula: A Vanishing People in the New Hebrides* (George Routledge & Sons, 1934)

Chapter 10: The Hierarchy of our Brain

Full text of 'The Labyrinth' can be found: http://www.dianadurham.net/poems.html

Iain McGilchrist, *The Master and his Emissary: The Divided Brain and the Making of the Western World* (Yale University Press, 2009)

Chapter 11: How We Malfunction

George Eliot quote from *Middlemarch*, Chapter 42

Full text of 'Light Way' can be found: http://www.dianadurham. net/poems.html

Lama Anagarika Govinda, *Foundations of Tibetan Mysticism* (BI Publications PVT Ltd., 1994 Indian reprint)

Chapter 12: Inflation

Krishnamurti quote from *The Collected Works Volume XIII*, 'Saanen, 1st Public Talk, 22nd July 1962'

'Structural Trap' from *Between Two Worlds* (Chrysalis Poetry, 2014)

Lama Anagarika Govinda, *Foundations of Tibetan Mysticism* (BI Publications PVT Ltd., 1994 Indian reprint)

David Bohm, *Unfolding Meaning: A Weekend of Dialogue*, edited by Donald Factor (Foundation House Publications, 1985)

Chapter 13: The Fall in Consciousness

Diabolic by Jay Ramsay from Monuments (Waterloo Press, 2014) also available as an ebook.

Lama Anagarika Govinda, *Foundations of Tibetan Mysticism* (BI Publications PVT Ltd., 1994 Indian reprint)

Chapter 14: Dust

Excerpt from 'Metanoia', Part 17 of 'Summerland' by Jay Ramsay from *Monuments* (Waterloo Press, 2014), also available as an e-book.

Ken Wilber, *A Brief History of Everything* (Shambhala, revised 2000 edition)

John Anthony West, *Serpent in the Sky: The High Wisdom of Ancient Egypt* (Quest Books, 1993)

Chapter 15: Money-Scapes

Excerpt from 'Walk In Somewhere and Return', poem first published in *Parabola* magazine, Summer 2012

David Bohm, *Wholeness and the Implicate Order* (Ark Paperbacks, 1983)

HRH Charles, Prince of Wales, *Harmony: A New Way of Looking at Our World* (HarperCollins, 2010)

Chapter 16: Violence, Spin, Madness, Guns

'The Dark King' from *Between Two Worlds* (Chrysalis Poetry, 2014)

For an in-depth exploration of the meaning of the Wounded King and the Wasteland from the grail myth see my first non-fiction book, *The Return of King Arthur: Completing the Quest for Wholeness, Inner Strength, and Self-Knowledge*, (Tarcher/Penguin, 2004), now in the process of being turned into an e-book – my website will have details: www.dianadurham.net.

Richard J. Godwin, 'The Shard – monument to the real rulers of London', *London Evening Standard*, 4 July 2012 (https://www.standard.co.uk/comment/comment/the-shard-monument-to-the-real-rulers-of-london-7908092.html)

Chapter 17: The Ring of Dark Belief

David Bohm, from a lecture given at UC Berkeley, 1977

Chapter 18: False Certainty

Asimov quote from his novel *Foundation* (Gnome Press, 1951)

'It Could Have Been Different' excerpt from *To the End of the Night* (Northwoods Press, 2004)

For some of the insights about and account of George W. Bush, I drew on Bob Woodward's four volume biography, particularly *State of Denial: Bush at War, Part III* (Simon & Schuster, 2006).

Chapter 19: Kennedy & the King Arthur Myth

Schumacher quote from 'Small is Beautiful', an essay in *The Radical*

Humanist, Vol. 37, No. 5 (August 1973), p. 22

'New Bearings' excerpt from *To the End of the Night* (Northwoods Press, 2004)

Robert Kennedy, *Thirteen Days: A Memoir of the Cuban Missile Crisis* (WW Norton, 1969) (one year after his assassination)

Thirteen Days (2000), docudrama directed by Roger Donaldson

Chapter 20: A Round Table

Round Table quote from *The Quest of the Holy Grail*, edited by Pauline Maud Matarasso, London (Penguin Classics, 1969)

'The Coronet' excerpt from *To the End of the Night* (Northwoods Press, 2004)

David Bohm, *Unfolding Meaning: A Weekend of Dialogue*, edited by Donald Factor (Foundation House Publications, 1985)

For quotes and the story about Cesar Chavez and the United Farm Workers, see *The Power of Collective Wisdom and the Trap of Collective Folly* by Alan Briskin, Sheryl Erickson, Tom Callanan and John Ott (Berrett-Koehler Publishers, Inc., 2009).

Chapter 21: Dialogue & Collective Coherence

'No Temple' excerpt from *To the End of the Night* (Northwoods Press, 2004)

King Hussein I quote from Address to the Seventh Organization of the Islamic Conference Summit, Casablanca, Morocco, December 14, 1994.

William Isaacs, *Dialogue and the art of thinking together* (Currency/Doubleday, 1999), also referencing the work of Otto Scharmer

Otto Scharmer, from his executive summary of *Theory U: Leading from the Future as It Emerges*

Chapter 22: Initiation by the Group Presence

Excerpt from *Awakening Osiris: A New Translation of the Egyptian Book of the Dead* by Normandi Ellis (Phanes Press, 1988)

'Finding Your Voice', http://www.dianadurham.net/poems.html

Craig Hamilton's article 'Come Together! The Power of Collective Intelligence' in *What is Enlightenment* magazine, Issue 25, May-July 2004

See also Ria Baeck and *Collective Presencing*, book and website.

And Art of Hosting website & practitioners.

Chapter 23: Inside the Grail Castle

'Here Comes the Meaning of it All' from *Between Two Worlds* (Chrysalis Poetry, 2014)

For an in-depth exploration of the meaning of the grail story see my first non-fiction book, *The Return of King Arthur: Completing the Quest for Wholeness, Inner Strength, and Self-Knowledge*, (Tarcher/Penguin, 2004), now in the process of being turned into an e-book – my website will have details: www.dianadurham.net.

See also our YouTube channel, Gandy Dancer Films, with the animated retelling of the Grail story, *Perceval & the Grail* and series of talks by me, *Coherence & the Grail Myth*.

Chapter 24: Joining the Worlds

'Confession' by Jay Ramsay, first published in *Amethyst Review*, edited by Sarah Law, February 2018

Sir Arthur Eddington, *The Nature of the Physical World*, Gifford Lectures of 1927 (Cambridge University Press, First Edition, 1928)

Acknowledgments

The teachings of Lloyd Meeker and Martin Exeter form the first foundation of the insights in this book, and I am thankful for their work, and for the community drawn around them, many of whom remain friends today. I am grateful also for the work of Donald Factor and Peter Garrett in drawing together the first dialogue conference with theoretical physicist David Bohm, as well as subsequent dialogue gatherings. Listening to Bohm talk was electrifying, and I am lucky to have been in the presence of one of the 20th century's great geniuses. I am grateful as well for the support over many years of poet and colleague Jay Ramsay, who has long been a visionary when postmodern and reductionist worldviews were the literary fashion and who has graciously let me quote from some of his poems. And I want to thank my friend Don Tirabassi, who encouraged and worked with me to turn the grail myth into an audioplay, during which process my understanding of the story continued to develop and the insights in this book to crystallize. I am very appreciative of the efforts of Sarah Jane Freymann who read various drafts of this book in the long process of distilling its essential content and helped suggest the title. Finally, I want to express my love and appreciation for my family: my husband Jon who supports me emotionally and practically, and for my two amazing children, now young adults, Raphael and Aidyn, of whom I am so proud.

More Information about the Author and Her Work

The Return of King Arthur: Completing the Quest for Wholeness,
Inner Strength, and Self-Knowledge

Interprets the legends of King Arthur and the quest for the Grail chalice to trace both the individual path to wholeness and the emergence of a new paradigm of collective leadership in today's society.

'The Grail Myth is probably the last great offering of the collective unconscious and is the most pertinent of all its treasures. We are in the midst of this great story, all of us agonizing from the fisher king wound, driven to find the Grail Castle, tugging at the sword maddeningly stuck in the stone. To find the modern relevance of this story is to set one instantly on his own intimate search.

Diana Durham does masterful work in bringing this jewel of the Western world into just such relevance; she makes it possible to begin one's own grail quest in terms understandable for our present mentality.'

Robert A. Johnson, D. Hum, author of *He, She, Inner Work, We* and *Owning Your Own Shadow*

Jeremy P. Tarcher/Penguin 2004, Non-fiction
ISBN 1-58542-297-5

The Curve of the Land

Set in 1980s Britain against the backdrop of ecological crisis, *The Curve of the Land* is about our modern relationship with the Earth, which in this case is represented by the landscapes of western Britain. Jessica, an ardent but unfulfilled activist, joins a tour of megalithic sites hoping to find renewal from relationship burn-out and a sterile work environment. The characters on the tour are a good cross section of the way 'new age', occult and mystical threads got grafted on to the more intellectual or 'respectable' British stock, throwing up eccentric cameos of people and comic situations. The mysterious atmosphere of the stones and her growing attraction for the charismatic tour leader builds to a final shamanic climax in the wilds of West Penwith, Cornwall.

'... [this] thoughtful, passionate, and sometimes edgy novel is a love story, a coming of (middle) age novel, a search for identity and community, a meditation on the environment, and a philosophical inquiry into the relevance of ancient beliefs to our own time and sensibility.'

Ernest Hebert, author of *The Dogs of March*, Professor of English, Dartmouth College

Skylight Press 2015, Fiction

ISBN: 978-1-908011-92-3

Sea of Glass

First full-length collection of poems.

'To convey deep feeling in language that amplifies that feeling on every reading is to go beyond language towards a deeper communication than words can ever convey. The intonation and expression of the poet comes with each stanza, to the extent that the reader absorbs the words as his/her own, that is the gift of the poet. Diana has that gift.'

Kindred Spirit Magazine, UK

The Diamond Press, London, 1989, Poetry

ISBN 0-948684-06-2

To the End of the Night

One of three winners of the Northwoods Press 2003 annual poetry competition. The poems trace the poet's journey from England to America, and a parallel journey through the heart to a place of renewed vision and synthesis of understanding.

'A political, poetic, and philosophic descendant of Blake, she names the nature and architecture of places where violence rhymes with benevolence. Here in these poems, at the end of the night, "thought [is] overtaken / by sensation" and we must greet the day

willing to be "taken hostage / by uncertainty."'
Alice B. Fogel, author of *Be That Empty*, New Hampshire Poet
Laureate
Northwoods Press 2004, Poetry
ISBN 0-89002-374-3

Between Two Worlds

A series of 50 sonnets explores the way new meaning in thought
and insight is woven because of the relationship between inner
and outer awareness.

The underlying understanding, with linkage to Tibetan Buddhist
thought, is that consciousness is the overlap between two dimensions or 'worlds', and creativity and inspired, generative action
spring out of this relationship in ourselves.

'Beautiful – your work speaks to me.'
Iain McGilchrist, author of *The Master and his Emissary: The Di-
vided Brain and the Making of the Western World*
Chrysalis Poetry pamphlet, 2012

See also: *Perceval & the Grail* in CD and downloadable form as an
audioplay as well as an animated series on YouTube: Perceval &
the Grail Part 1 Morgana's Retelling – YouTube (https://www.
youtube.com/watch?v=EGv8MiZkkFQ&t=3s). Her channel also
features a series of talks about *Coherence & the Grail Myth*: https://
youtu.be/uNG1Oceom_A.

About the author

Following a degree in English Literature from University College,
London, I took the 'path less travelled' and became involved in intentional community in England, the United States and Canada. In
the 1980s I was invited to explore dialogue and collective intelligence with the late theoretical physicist David Bohm. Out of these

experiences I began a deep inquiry into the possibility that our current ecological and social crises are reflections of a prevailing dysfunctional identity and consciousness as human beings. Realizing that the same insights are embodied in the Arthurian and grail myths, exemplified by the Wounded King and the Wasteland Kingdom, I explored their meaning in depth in my first non-fiction book *The Return of King Arthur: Completing the Quest for Wholeness, Inner Strength, and Self-Knowledge* to which this is a companion book.

In London I was a member of the London poetry performance group Angels of Fire, appearing with them at the Royal Festival Hall's Voice Box. In New Hampshire I founded '3 Voices', three women writers who received state funding and performed statewide. I am a mother of two extraordinary young adults; am British but have lived in the US for the past 20 years. Between 2011/2012 I was a visiting scholar at the WSRC of Brandeis University. Additionally, I give talks and workshops on the grail myth, many sponsored by the NH Humanities Council (in the US), as well as national and international women's groups and business executive leadership training courses.

As well as writing books, I collaborate with my husband as writer/producer of other documentary films. Our current project is a series of short films, *Making Sense*, featuring writers, psychologists and practical visionaries whose work opens up a new understanding of how our brain and powers of consciousness affect our lives and shape the wider culture. For the first film we talked to psychiatrist Dr Iain McGilchrist, author of *The Master and his Emissary: The Divided Brain and the Making of Western Culture*: Gandy Dancer Films - YouTube - YouTube, (https://www.youtube.com/channel/UCi45eevINsjyn8ZtFbye2kQ).

In all my work, including poetry, I draw on both archetype and the numinous presence of the natural world to explore why our deeper identity is the root of creativity and the visionary power of imagination. Both – I believe – are essential forces in the renewal of culture.

O-BOOKS

SPIRITUALITY

O is a symbol of the world, of oneness and unity; this eye
represents knowledge and insight. We publish titles on general
spirituality and living a spiritual life. We aim to inform
and help you on your own journey in this life.
If you have enjoyed this book, why not tell other readers
by posting a review on your preferred book site? Recent
bestsellers from O-Books are:

Heart of Tantric Sex
Diana Richardson
Revealing Eastern secrets of deep love and intimacy to Western
couples.
Paperback: 978-1-90381-637-0 ebook: 978-1-84694-637-0

Crystal Prescriptions
The A-Z guide to over 1,200 symptoms and their healing crystals
Judy Hall
The first in the popular series of six books, this handy
little guide is packed as tight as a pill-bottle with crystal
remedies for ailments.
Paperback: 978-1-90504-740-6 ebook: 978-1-84694-629-5

Take Me To Truth
Undoing the Ego
Nouk Sanchez, Tomas Vieira
The best-selling step-by-step book on shedding the Ego,
using the teachings of *A Course In Miracles*.
Paperback: 978-1-84694-050-7 ebook: 978-1-84694-654-7

The 7 Myths about Love...Actually!
The journey from your HEAD to the HEART of your SOUL
Mike George
Smashes all the myths about LOVE.
Paperback: 978-1-84694-288-4 ebook: 978-1-84694-682-0

The Holy Spirit's Interpretation of the New Testament
A course in Understanding and Acceptance
Regina Dawn Akers
Following on from the strength of *A Course In Miracles*, NTI
teaches us how to experience the love and oneness of God.
Paperback: 978-1-84694-085-9 ebook: 978-1-78099-083-5

The Message of A Course In Miracles
A translation of the text in plain language
Elizabeth A. Cronkhite
A translation of *A Course in Miracles* into plain, everyday
language for anyone seeking inner peace. The companion
volume, *Practicing A Course In Miracles*, offers practical lessons
and mentoring.
Paperback: 978-1-84694-319-5 ebook: 978-1-84694-642-4

Thinker's Guide to God
Peter Vardy
An introduction to key issues in the philosophy of religion.
Paperback: 978-1-90381-622-6

Your Simple Path
Find happiness in every step
Ian Tucker
A guide to helping us reconnect with what is really important
in our lives.
Paperback: 978-1-78279-349-6 ebook: 978-1-78279-348-9

365 Days of Wisdom
Daily Messages To Inspire You Through The Year
Dadi Janki
Daily messages which cool the mind, warm the heart and guide
you along your journey.
Paperback: 978-1-84694-863-3 ebook: 978-1-84694-864-0

Body of Wisdom
Women's Spiritual Power and How it Serves
Hilary Hart
Bringing together the dreams and experiences of women across
the world with today's most visionary spiritual teachers.
Paperback: 978-1-78099-696-7 ebook: 978-1-78099-695-0

Dying to Be Free
From Enforced Secrecy to Near Death to True Transformation
Hannah Robinson
After an unexpected accident and near-death experience, Hannah
Robinson found herself radically transforming her life, while
a remarkable new insight altered her relationship with her father,
a practising Catholic priest.
Paperback: 978-1-78535-254-6 ebook: 978-1-78535-255-3

The Ecology of the Soul
A Manual of Peace, Power and Personal Growth for Real People
in the Real World
Aidan Walker
Balance your own inner Ecology of the Soul to regain your
natural state of peace, power and wellbeing.
Paperback: 978-1-78279-850-7 ebook: 978-1-78279-849-1

Not I, Not other than I
The Life and Teachings of Russel Williams
Steve Taylor, Russel Williams
The miraculous life and inspiring teachings of one of the World's
greatest living Sages.
Paperback: 978-1-78279-729-6 ebook: 978-1-78279-728-9

On the Other Side of Love
A Woman's Unconventional Journey Towards Wisdom
Muriel Maufroy
When life has lost all meaning, what do you do?
Paperback: 978-1-78535-281-2 ebook: 978-1-78535-282-9

Practicing A Course In Miracles
A Translation of the Workbook in Plain Language and With
Mentoring Notes
Elizabeth A. Cronkhite
The practical second and third volumes of The Plain-Language
A Course In Miracles.
Paperback: 978-1-84694-403-1 ebook: 978-1-78099-072-9

Quantum Bliss
The Quantum Mechanics of Happiness, Abundance, and Health
George S. Mentz
Quantum Bliss is the breakthrough summary of success and
spirituality secrets that customers have been waiting for.
Paperback: 978-1-78535-203-4 ebook: 978-1-78535-204-1

The Upside Down Mountain
Mags MacKean
A must-read for anyone weary of chasing success and happiness
– one woman's inspirational journey swapping the uphill slog
for the downhill slope.
Paperback: 978-1-78535-171-6 ebook: 978-1-78535-172-3

Your Personal Tuning Fork
The Endocrine System
Deborah Bates
Discover your body's health secret, the endocrine system,
and 'twang' your way to sustainable health!
Paperback: 978-1-84694-503-8 ebook: 978-1-78099-697-4

Readers of ebooks can buy or view any of these bestsellers
by clicking on the live link in the title. Most titles are published
in paperback and as an ebook. Paperbacks are available in
traditional bookshops. Both print and ebook formats are
available online.

Find more titles and sign up to our readers' newsletter at
http://www.johnhuntpublishing.com/mind-body-spirit

Follow us on Facebook at https://www.facebook.com/OBooks/
and Twitter at https://twitter.com/obooks